My First Book of Java

RAVIT SHARMA

ISBN: 197385547X

ISBN-13: 978-1973855477

DEDICATION

To my parents, Rohit and Rashmi, and my brother, Rohan.

TRADEMARKS

Java™ and Oracle™ are registered trademarks of Oracle and/or its affiliates.

The "Eclipse" name and logo are the intellectual property of the Eclipse Foundation.

C++™

C#™

Windows™

Mac™

Linux™

PREFACE

The motivation behind this book is to provide a beginner programmer with an introduction to the Java language. It requires very little to no experience with computer programming and contains all you need to commence basic programming in Java.

This book is intended for all beginning programmers, from students in middle school to an adult starting in the world of programming. I have tried keeping the language used in this book relatively straightforward to allow a reader to comprehend the text with ease. Diagrams are also included throughout the book to aid the reader in understanding the covered material.

This book comprises nine chapters. At the end of each chapter except the last are programming questions that the reader can use to test and clarify his knowledge of that chapter.

Chapter 1 – Getting Started

This chapter starts off with an introduction to Java, as well as its history and origins. It also demonstrates how a programmer can get started with programming with Java. This chapter also holds a tutorial for every programmer's first program, Hello World.

Chapter 2 – Foundation

This chapter provides the basis for programming in Java. It elaborates on the basics of variables, control statements, and various operators used while programming.

Chapter 3 – Object-oriented Programming

This chapter covers what objects are, what object-oriented programming is, as well as the elements of object-oriented programming: polymorphism, inheritance, and encapsulation.

Chapter 4 – Classes and Interfaces

This chapter includes more detail on elements of object-oriented programming, specifically, classes and interfaces. It covers more detail on classes, and introduces interfaces.

Chapter 5 – Threads

This chapter introduces concurrency and threads in Java to the reader.

Chapter 6 – Exceptions

This chapter discusses the exceptional conditions that arise during execution of the program. It includes why they happen, their difference from errors, and how the programmer can manage them.

Chapter 7 – Nested Classes

This chapter explores the concept of nested classes, a class within a class, to the user.

Chapter 8 – Libraries

This chapter introduces libraries to the programmer. It covers what they are, what they comprise, as well as the most commonly used packages in the Java standard libraries.

Chapter 9 – Putting it all Together

This last chapter contains a collection of programs for the programmer to attempt on his own, and incorporates some of the concepts the reader has learned. There are no questions at the end this chapter.

To get the most out of this book, you should thoroughly read and understand the chapters of this book in order. The information covered by each chapter often builds on topics covered in preceding chapters. Even if you are not new to computer programming, I recommend that you still glance through the introductory chapters (Chapters 1, 2, 3) and complete the questions at the end of the chapter to ensure that you have correctly understood the concepts covered in the chapter. If you do this, you will have learned the basics of Java by the end of this book.

I have used two fonts for the body of the text. One is a standard font, used for explanations in the majority of the book, and the other is code font, used for demonstrations of a program or just a simple instruction, the words of the computer language. Here is a sample, so you know what to expect from this book.

STANDARD FONT

```
CODE FONT
```

Italicized code font will be used to represent something that is a placeholder for actual code. Please note that the italicized font will not compile.

```
CODE PLACEHOLDER FONT
```

Keep in mind while reading this book that programming is often time-consuming. At first, you may find yourself struggling to identify a simple problem. The only way you can improve is through practice. Remember to practice patience while coding and never give up.

Hopefully, you will find reading this book rewarding in that it gives you the knowledge you need to start programming in Java. Although it does not cover all topics of the Java language, it certainly will help set up the foundation you need to learn more about it.

Throughout this book, I have tried to ensure that the content of this book is lucid and accurate. Despite my efforts, it is possible that I have made an error in this book. In the case that you catch a mistake in my writing or have any other comments/suggestions, please feel free to contact me at myfirstbookofjava@gmail.com.

For more information regarding this book, please visit myfirstbookofjava.com. On this url, you will find:

1. All the source code for examples in this book available for download
2. A list of errata in this book
3. Solution to selected problems
4. Other testimonials, pictures and current information

CONTENTS

ACKNOWLEDGEMENTS

I am grateful to all those who have helped me in the creation of this book, especially my parents, for being very patient, helpful, encouraging and supportive along the way.

1 GETTING STARTED

Let's get ready to program in Java! This chapter will cover a basic history and background of Java, Java's applications in the real world, how to get ready for coding in Java, our first program: Hello World, as well as some tips to proofread your code.

What is Java?

Java is a very widespread programming language. It can be used to create almost anything, from Applets (small applications) to game consoles. Android, a popular operating system for mobile devices runs on code written in Java. Let's first get familiar with some of Java's basics.

History of Java

James Gosling is the main creator of the original Java language. At the time, he worked for a company called Sun Microsystems. However, this company was later acquired by another company called Oracle Corp. Oracle now owns the programming language. Ever since the beginning of Java, more and more programmers have begun to use this programming language. In addition, Java is a constantly evolving language, meaning that it keeps changing. Different versions of Java continue to be released whenever the creators feel that changes are required.

Terminology

Before we get into coding, you should know some terms of programming. These words are often used by programmers and will be used throughout the rest of the book.

Computer Programming Language

A computer programming language is simply a method of communication through which we give the computer instructions. There are several computer programming languages that exist, such as C++, Java, and Python, but this book teaches you how to write programs in Java programming language, much like a grammar book tells you how to correctly communicate in English.

Code

Code consists of instructions written in a computer language. The Java programs that you will write consist of code. Code is what you probably imagine when you think of programming.

```
void co    tFile(fina   yntaxNod   n) thro   CodeExcept
for (It    or ite=sn.g  hildren   createI  ator();ite
   fi     SyntaxNode c    (Synta  ode)ite  xt();
   fi     Rule r le = c  etRule  ;
   if(    E_PACK GE==ru   {
   }el    ck = c  .getCh   ByRule( ULE_REF  getTok  sChars
          if(RU  IMPORT  ule){
          /TODO handle st  c and
          inal SyntaxNode  n = cn.getCh  ByRule(RULE_IMPO
          inal C  s fullN  e = ccn.getT  nsChars
          final C  s[] par  = fullName.  it('.')
```

There are several other instances of code in the Java language. Bytecode and binary code are also different types of code. Let's take an analogy comparing programming languages with human languages. English is an example of a human language and Java is an example of a programming language. If English were a programming language, then sentences and paragraphs would make up its code.

Program

A program is simply a series of instructions given to the computer.

A program is written in something called a file. A file is simply data that is stored in the memory of the computer. Every file has a name, but no two files in a single directory can have the same name. When you want to execute a program, you execute a specific file.

Main Method

In Java, each file contains one block of code called a class that holds nearly all the code of a program. The instructions that the computer executes are written in a section of the class called the "main method". Not all classes contain a main method, but if there is no main method present in the class, the computer has no instructions to follow, and therefore cannot run the program. You can only execute a file if there is a main method present in its class. This contains the instructions for the computer to execute. A program stops after all the instructions in the main method are done being executed. However, due to Java's object-oriented style, there is code that exists outside the main method as well.

Execute

To execute means to put into action. This term usually takes a program or a single instruction as its direct object. Executing a program means telling the computer to follow the instructions written in a program. Executing a line of code means telling the computer to follow the instruction written in that line of code. You can tell the computer to execute a program, but not a line of code. There is usually only one instruction per line of code.

While you are writing the instructions for the computer, the computer does not execute that statement as soon as it is written. Instead, you need to expressly tell the computer when you want it to execute your program.

Run

Run means the same thing as execute. To run a program means telling the computer to start executing the instructions of that program. However, "run" is usually only used in the context of an entire program. For example, you can run a program, but not a single line of code.

How Java Works

One big distinguishing factor about Java is what happens to the code from the moment it is run to when it stops. Let's look at what the computer does differently when running Java code.

Traditional Programming Languages

First, I should make it clear that computers (more specifically, their CPUs) do not directly read and understand the programming languages we write in: Java, C++, HTML, or any other language. When you run a computer program, the computer cannot immediately set off to read the code that you write. Instead, it must take an extra step. This is true for almost all programming languages. Here are what traditional programming languages (not Java) do.

Computers understand a language called machine code, written in just two numbers, 0 and 1. Our programming language must be converted into machine code before the computer can understand it.

Machine code is a special language that only computers can understand. (you can learn it too, but it would be painstakingly meticulous for you to do so.) This is because the language of computers is only in 0s and 1s (called binary). That's right! Computers only understand this language made up of just two numbers. In addition, every program turns into different machine code depending on the computer. The machine code for a program varies depending on the computer. However, the output does not change.

So, for computers to read and carry out your instructions, they first must get the programming language translated into machine language. The CPU of the computer then executes the machine language. (By the way, computers are fast. Most programs can be executed within a split second.)

Because of this close relationship between the language and machine code, a program often has to be changed to be run on different machines. For example, a program on a Mac may not run the way you expect on a Windows machine. As a result, it is a headache for program developers to create applications on different platforms, as the programs is different.

As you will see, Java solves this problem in a clever way.

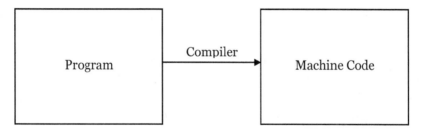

Java

Java, on the other hand, does something different that gives it some of its unique features, such as architecture-neutrality and platform independence. More of these features will be discussed shortly. However, speed is one cost of Java's JVM. JVMs themselves tend to be much slower than other compilers. Despite this, JVMs are still very fast.

Much like with other programming languages, the computer does not directly understand the Java programming language.

JVM Execution

The CPU executes traditional programming languages, such as C++ and Smalltalk. You can think of the CPU like the brain of the computer. It turns the programming language into machine code using a compiler and then executes it. Java is different. A program called the Java Virtual Machine (JVM) runs Java. The JVM is a program that acts like the CPU and executes instructions.

Instead of converting Java code straight into machine language, Java first turns its code into an intermediate level called bytecode. Bytecode is another language like machine code. However, only the owners of Java (Oracle Corp.) have the formula for converting Java programming language into bytecode. They do not tell the formula to anyone else. Instead, they created the Java Compiler to turn a Java program into bytecode, and the JVM to execute the bytecode.

The benefit of bytecode is that it is universal across all platforms (a platform is the hardware and software that make up a machine). This means that the bytecode for a Java program is the same everywhere regardless of the platform running the program. On the contrary, several other programming languages often have to change their code to reflect the platform.

The Java Virtual Machine then takes care of converting the bytecode into the machine language (different depending on the CPU). Unlike other languages like C++, the byte code for a programming language does not change depending on the processor.

JIT Compiler

The Just in Time (JIT) Compiler is a component of the Java Development Kit that increases the execution speed of a program. The JIT Compiler comes along with the Java Development Kit and is a much faster alternative to the JVM itself. The JIT compiler is almost as fast as a C++ compiler. (I use C++ because it is a close relative of the Java language.)

The JIT compiler works by compiling the bytecode of a program into machine code and then executing it. Thus, the JIT only needs to compile the bytecode once before it has the machine code for the program. It can then run the machine language as many times as you like, which is much faster than running the bytecode itself. On the other hand, the JVM executes the bytecode when you run it.

Buzzwords

Simple

Java is simple. The creators intended for this language to be straightforward and clear. As a result, Java has many features that make it straightforward, such as its organization of programs into classes, which we will discuss later.

Secure

Java is also safe. Running or downloading Java applications are safe in it does not harm the computer. These Java applications are also run in the Java Virtual Machine, not in the CPU itself. Java code is converted into bytecode and run in the JVM, which verifies the bytecode and prevents a

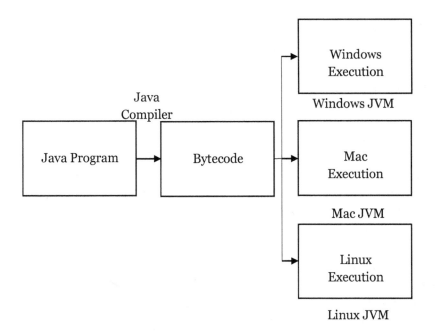

virus from accessing and harming the rest of the computer.

Portable

Since Java first converts code into bytecode, it can easily move from platform to platform over the Internet. Since many types of platforms with different binary code instructions access the Internet, Java allows bytecode to be used over the Internet so that any platform can execute the same bytecode.

Object-oriented

Java is an object-oriented language, meaning that its programs are organized in classes. Objects can then be created from those classes to model situations in real life. You will learn more about this in the next chapter.

Robust

Unlike C++, a close relative of the Java language, Java handles its own memory meaning that the programmer does not have to worry about taking too much memory and cleaning up after himself.

Multithreaded

Java is a language that allows the programmer to perform many tasks at the same time (multithreaded language). A thread is simply a sequence of instructions given to the computer that need to be done (single threaded). You can do this in Java, when making a regular program. But what if you want to do many things at the same time? Java also allows you to do this by creating and running multiple threads. More on threads will be covered in a later chapter.

Architecture-neutral

The code for certain programming languages changes depending on the platform. For example, two different programs may be required to produce the same output on, for example, a MacBook and an HP Laptop.

You can write and run a program in Java regardless of the architecture of your computer. Java works by first converting Java code into a universal bytecode (the same bytecode can be run across all computers, regardless of their architecture). Then, the Java Virtual Machine (JVM) takes care of converting that bytecode into machine code specific for each platform. The fact that Java can be run across all computers regardless of their architecture makes it architecture-neutral. This feature of Java is commonly referred to as "write once, run anywhere".

Interpreted

Java is interpreted, not compiled. To compile means to directly translate from a programming language to binary code for a specific machine. To interpret means to first translate a programming language into something else, and then "interpret" (translate) that intermediary code into machine language, written in binary code. Java first turns its code into bytecode and then interprets the meaning of that bytecode using the Java Virtual Machine (JVM) depending on the platform.

High Performance

Java is also high-performance. Even though Java takes an extra step by first converting code into bytecode, the JVM also comes equipped with a Just-In-Time Compiler. This compiler turns bytecode of a program into instructions directly executable by the computer as opposed to direct execution of bytecode (in the JVM). As a result, the JIT compiler can execute programs almost as quickly as a C++ compiler.

Distributed

Java is distributed because several computers connected by means of the Internet can interact with each other. Parts of a Java program can execute on different CPU/cores on different machines or on multiple CPU/cores of the same machine.

Dynamic

Java programs are dynamic, meaning that they keep changing. Java is dynamic because it may not know what code to execute until the program runs. For example, the same program may have a different outcome depending on the setting in which it is run. Java does not know what is going to happen until the program is executed, which is why it is dynamic. This feature also gives rise to exceptional conditions, runtime problems that occur.

Uses

Java has a variety of applications. For example, Android, a popular operating system for mobile devices runs on Java. Java can also be used to create applications and Applets, such as a text editor or a video game. Applets especially, are very popular on the Internet, mainly because they are architecture neutral. If you attentively read until the end of this book, even you will be able to create simple Applets and applications in Java.

What makes Java different?

So, what makes Java different from the other programming languages, such as C++? Well, one reason that it attracted several programmers during the late nineties rather than C++ is its success in the Internet. Java wasn't originally designed for the Internet, but the creators soon realized that Java would also work well there, especially since it was a new concept and its popularity was dramatically increasing. As a result, Java has several features that contribute to its suitability for the Internet. To understand these, we need to understand a little more about how it works.

Platform Independence

Unlike the C languages, Java is not compiled. Instead, it is interpreted. It is first converted into bytecode, and then executed by a Java Virtual Machine (JVM), as opposed to solely the processor. A JVM is a program on a computer that compiles and executes Java programs. The advantage of a JVM is that the code of the program doesn't have to change depending on the processor; the JVM takes care of converting the byte code into assembly language. However, the disadvantage is that there is an extra step:

converting the code into bytecode. Overall, Java takes away the headache of changing the code from processor to processor away from developers.

To understand platform independence, we first need to learn what a platform is. A platform is like a computer. Examples of platforms include HP Laptops and MacBooks. Every platform has different hardware (physical components), such as keyboards, charging cables, and battery types. An HP laptop's charging cable is different from a MacBook's. As a result, the CPU (brain of the computer) carries out different instructions depending on the type of platform.

These instructions given to the computer are written only in 0s and 1s. This is called binary code. The computer (specifically the CPU) only understands instructions in binary code. All platforms read binary code in the same way, but they need to do different things to accomplish the same task. The language is the same; the instructions are different.

What if you want to let a friend run a program you made on his computer? You can't send the program in the form of binary code, as this will not work on your friend's computer (since the binary code for a program is different on each platform). You can't give him the code for your program either, because he might steal your code. At this point, there isn't much you can do. The creators of Java attempted to solve this in their programming language. Java is platform independent, meaning that you can write code once and run it on any platform.

What is a platform?

To understand platform independence, we first need to learn what a platform is. A platform refers to the unique hardware of computer. Examples of platforms include HP Laptops and MacBook. An HP Laptop has a different platform than a MacBook, but two MacBook Airs of the same model have the same platform.

What makes platforms different?

Every platform has different hardware (physical components), such as keyboards, charging cables, and battery types. An HP laptop's charging cable is different from a MacBook's. As a result, the CPU (brain of the computer) carries out different instructions depending on the type of platform.

These instructions given to the computer are written only in 0s and 1s. This is called binary code. The computer (specifically the CPU) only understands instructions in binary code. All platforms read binary code in the same way, but they need to do different things to accomplish the same task. The language is the same; the instructions are different.

What is platform independence?

Platform independence is a language's ability to be written once and then compiled and run the same way on any platform. Some programming languages need to be modified to work on different platforms, such as smartphones, tablets, and desktops, to better suit each platform's needs. For example, unlike desktops, there is no mouse on a phone, so a program initially designed for a desktop may need to be changed. If a program needs to be changed to reflect different hardware, it is platform dependent.

If a language is platform independent, the same program in that language can be run on any platform.

Why is Java Platform Independent?

Java can be compiled once and run on any platform. This can be done because of the way Java code is compiled and executed.

Unlike most other computer programming languages, such as C++, which compile code in their language to machine code, Java converts its code into something called bytecode. Bytecode is an intermediate level used when running the program. Unlike machine code, which is different for different platforms, bytecode is universal, meaning that the exact same bytecode can be run the same way on all platforms.

Since Java is compiled into universal bytecode, it can be compiled once and run on any platform. As a result, it is written without regard to the platform, unifying code across all platforms. For the most part, the platform of the computer does not affect the way one programs. Unlike other programming languages, Java is written once, compiled into universal bytecode, and is then executed. Java bytecode is executed by a program called a Java Virtual Machine (JVM). This program simply takes care of executing the bytecode. Every computer has a different JVM that executes bytecode differently for each platform. In other words, the differences among the platforms are handled not in the code but by the JVM in execution.

Object-Oriented

Java is object-oriented, meaning that it is a programming language centered around the creation and interaction of objects. In computer science, an object is simply an instance of a class. This concept will be discussed in more detail in a subsequent chapter.

The object-oriented aspect of Java is beneficial because an object can be created to represent virtually anything. For example, let's take an example of a car-manufacturing company. The company could use a computer program to keep track of all their cars. For every car they manufacture, they could create objects of a "car" with different properties, such as color, model, and serial number. Similarly, this idea can be extended to many other situations.

Java is certainly not the only object-oriented language. Others, such as C++, exist. However, Java's simplicity makes it an attractive choice.

Why Java?

Java is a great programming language for a couple of different reasons. Firstly, Java is platform independent, meaning that it can transfer from one computer to another without recompilation. Also, Java is a relatively simple language to learn. With determination and practice, you'll be able to master to master the basics of Java quickly.

Getting Ready to Code

To program in Java, you need two things: a Java Virtual Machine (JVM) and an Integrated Development Environment (IDE). A JVM turns Java code into executable binary code that can be read by the CPU of the computer. The

CPU is like the "brain" of a computer as it carries out most of its functions. An IDE provides you, the programmer, with several helpful tools that help you program. An IDE is not required to program. However, it is highly recommended and frankly quite useful.

Java Development Kit (JDK)

Java Compiler

The Java Compiler simply takes a Java program that you write and turns it into bytecode. Bytecode is the universal intermediate code that is executed by the JVM.

Java Virtual Machine (JVM)

You need a JVM (Java Virtual Machine) in order to run your program. You cannot execute a Java program unless you have a JVM. A JVM is simply responsible for executing the bytecode created by the Java Compiler. The Java Compiler translates your instructions to the computer, and the JVM is the program that goes through the list of instructions and executes them one by one.

Just-In-Time (JIT) Compiler

The Just-In-Time compiler compiles bytecode into machine code for that particular language. This provides a much faster alternative to executing the bytecode using the JVM

How to get the JDK

So, how can you get a Java Development Toolkit? Well, since Oracle Corp. owns the Java language, they also own the Java JDK. A JDK contains a Java Compiler, a Java Virtual Machine, and the JIT Compiler, among other components.

I recommend downloading the JDK from Oracle Corp. for two reasons. Firstly, they decide when to release a new version of the Java language, so you can depend on them to keep you up to date on the latest version of Java. In addition, they are the creators, so they can show you exactly what is different in the latest version of Java.

To download a Java JDK from Oracle Corp., first go to the following website: http://www.oracle.com/technetwork/java/javase/downloads/index.html, and click "JDK Download." This will redirect you to a page with a list of the latest Java JDKs for different operating systems (OS) to choose from. Choose your computer's operating system from the list titled "Java SE Development Kit 8u131" and download and install the JVM.[1]

Integrated Development Environment (IDE)

An integrated development environment is also helpful while programming in Java. An IDE is simply an application that provides features that are helpful while programming. For example, IDEs contain a debugger, a tool that is used to identify flaws in a program. In addition, IDEs are very helpful in identifying syntactical errors and solving formatting issues.

Like a JVM, an IDE can also be downloaded from the Internet. There are several IDEs available, and you can choose to download whichever one you wish; they all serve the same fundamental purpose.

---

[1] At the time that this book is published JDK 8 is the most recent version of Java. However, the language is constantly changing, so you should download the latest released JDK.

From my experience in programming with Java, I have found Eclipse to be very helpful. If you also want to download Eclipse, here is the link: https://www.eclipse.org/ide/. Simply click Java IDE under Desktop IDEs and find your computer's Operating System under Download Links on the right side of the page. As you program using an IDE, you will find that it proves to be very helpful.

First Sip of Java

Once you have your JVM and IDE set up, you are ready to begin programming. Usually, the first program that programmers write in a language is called "Hello World".

"Hello World" is a simple program in which the programmer writes code to print the text "Hello World" to the Console. The console in an IDE simply displays the output of the system. When one prints "Hello World" to the console, the phrase "Hello World" is displayed in the Console Window of the IDE.

The reason that people start off writing "Hello World" is tradition. You do not have to write the "Hello World" program as your first program; it is just the way people usually commence programming in a particular computer language.

Setting up a Program

Before we write any code, we need to understand how to set a program up such that a computer understands it.

Writing the "Hello World" program is relatively easy. To write a program, you first need to create a class. In Eclipse, you need to create a new project before creating this class. Once you have created a new project, you can create a new class in the src folder of the project. Here is how you create a class:

```
class CLASSNAME {
```

1 Getting Started

```
CLASS CONTENTS

}
```

Of course, you would have to replace CLASSNAME with the name of the class and CLASS CONTENTS with what you want to add to the class. We have to first create a class because that is how the computer knows what it has to read. A computer does not accept any instructions written outside the scope of a class. Scope is simply defined as the range of code covered by a certain class, method, or control statement. (These concepts will be covered later.) Whatever is in a class is its scope. The scope of a field is usually within the nearest pair of curly braces.

```
class example {

    CLASS CONTENTS

}
```

In the program we are about to write, the command telling the computer to write "Hello World" is within the scope of the class, and more specifically, the main method. The main method is the set of instructions that a computer reads first. When a program is run, the computer reads the instructions in the main method before anything else, and is required to run a class. Here is how you can create a main method:

```
public static void main (String [] args) {

    STATEMENTS

}
```

At first glance, this looks a bit complicated, but it will start to make more sense later. For now, though, just know that when the computer sees the main method, it first executes the code within its scope (i.e. the two curly braces). Remember that the main method goes within the scope of the class. That is the only way that it will be read by the computer. In the preceding code, STATEMENTS would be replaced with our instructions for the computer when we type the code.

Lastly, we must tell the computer to write "Hello World", which is the purpose of the program. This can be done using a simple print statement. Here's what that looks like:

```
System.out.print ("TEXT");
```

This statement tells the computer to print TEXT to the console. The computer prints the characters in the double quotations of the parentheses to the Console. If the command were

```
System.out.print ("Random Stuff ");
```

then the computer would print

```
Random Stuff
```

The parentheses of the command indicate that the information within them is to be displayed. The series of letters, numbers, whitespace, and/or symbols within the quotation marks is what the computer prints to the console. This continuation of characters is called a string (whatever is within the quotation marks – "Hello World", "Random Stuff". If not, the information inside the parentheses points to what should be displayed. Finally, remember that a statement always ends with a semicolon (;), just as it does in this case. The purpose of this is to tell the computer that the statement has completed and that there is no more to it.

In the Java Perspective of Eclipse, you should see the console toward the bottom. If you do not use Eclipse or still have trouble, the "Help" section of the menu should be of assistance.

Here's what the program should look like when we put everything together:

```
class Hello_World {

    public static void main (String[] args) {

        System.out.println ("Hello World");

    }

}
```

Here's what the console should look like:

```
Hello World
```

Proofreading Code

It is not uncommon for your program to not work the first time. Here are some tips you could use to make sure that your program works in the way that you intend. Double check to makes sure that your program is written exactly as above (the comments are optional). Keep in mind that Java is case-sensitive, meaning that to the computer, "book" is interpreted differently than "Book". Make sure that your program is written in a file with the same name as the class name (Hello_World). Also make sure that you are correctly compiling and executing your program. If make sure that all these things are correct, your program should work.

Debugging

Using the Debugger

The debugger is a helpful tool that you can use when detecting structural errors in a program.

Manually Debugging

One other useful tactic to find a structural flaw in a program is to think what you would do if you were the computer. All you need to do is understand what the program is doing, and follow the main method of the program, step by step.

Location of the Program

Make sure that the program you have written is typed in a file with the same name as the class. One file can only have one class, but one class can access other classes if they are in the same package.

Running the Program

Make sure that you run the program correctly. In Eclipse, you can do this by pressing "Ctrl" + F11 or by clicking Run (located in the menu). Also make sure that you are running the correct program. If not, you will not get the results you are expecting.

Case-Sensitivity

Keep in mind while programming that the Java language is case sensitive. That means that to the computer, "class" is not the same thing as "Class". As a result, you will need to make sure that your code does not have any incorrect capitalizations or lower-case letters. In the Hello World program, you can crosscheck your code with the sample code provided above.

Commands in Methods

Make sure that all the instructions that you give to the computer are inside methods. Commands to the computer are only executed if they are inside a method. However, you can have fields declared outside methods, but everything else goes inside the methods.

Flow of the Program

Lastly, it is possible that your program has a flaw, whether it be a syntactical or structural problem.

Syntactical

A syntactical flaw occurs when you make an error in typing the code, such as omitting a semicolon or not capitalizing a letter. This type of error prevents your program from being run successfully (because the computer does not understand what you are trying to say). It is relatively easy to detect a syntactical flaw. IDEs (including Eclipse) are able to point out most of these mistakes to you.

Semantic

On the other hand, semantic errors are harder to find. These happen when the code you have written can run without error, but does not give you the results you want. In this case, the computer understands what you are trying to say, but you tell the computer the wrong thing. IDEs do not point these out to you because there is no problem in identifying what the code says; you just tell the computer the wrong thing. For example, you might want to tell the computer to write a number five times, but your code tells the computer to write it six times. These types of errors can get very complicated. It is helpful to use a debugger when working with these types of errors because that allows you to pinpoint the location of the error and fix it.

Questions

Multiple Choice

1. Java is all of the following except

    a. Portable

    b. Platform-Independent

    c. Procedural

    d. Robust

2. Which command is used to print a string to the console?

    a. printf ();

    b. Console.WriteLine ();

    c. System.out.print ();

    d. stamp ();

3. Which of the following refers to a series of instructions given to the computer to execute?

    a. Program

    b. Class

    c. Code

    d. Programming language

4. Which of the following describes an issue that arises during compilation of a program?

    a. Problem

    b. Error

    c. Roadblock

    d. Stopper

5. Which of the following is NOT a factor that differentiates Java from other programming languages, such as C++?

    a. bytecode

    b. JVM

    c. Object-orientation

    d. Platform independence

6. What is the program responsible for executing Java bytecode?

    a. JVM

    b. JIT Compiler

    c. JDK

d.   Java Compiler

True/False

T	F	A class must have the same name as its file.
T	F	Java is not case-sensitive.
T	F	Java programs are executed by the CPU.
T	F	Java is slower than languages such as C++.
T	F	Most programs work for the first time, so there is no need to proofread code.
T	F	Sun Microsystems currently owns the Java language.
T	F	Programs consist of instructions for the computer written in a programming language.
T	F	Java needs to be rewritten to be run on different platforms.

T F	Comments are disregarded by the compiler.
T F	The Java Development Kit contains an Integrated Development Environment.

Free Response

1. Explain what happens to your program from the moment you run it to when it has finished execution. Make sure to include the keywords "Java code", "Java compiler", "bytecode", "JVM", and "platform" in your answer.

2. List out and explain three buzzwords of Java.

3. What is the JDK and why is it needed to program in Java? Make sure to include key components of the JDK.

2 FOUNDATION

To tell the computer what to do, we must write our code a certain way. If even one letter is not capitalized, the computer will not be able to do what you want it to do. For this reason, we must be very careful when we write code. For example, one important rule of thumb is that all statements end with a semicolon. The information in the following sections will let you know exactly how you need to write code to make the computer understand you.

Comments

What is a comment?

In computer science, a comment is a section of text in a program that is ignored by the JVM. Comments can be inserted anywhere in a program and are used for clarification for someone reading the code. At times, code can get really complicated and difficult to read. A programmer can add a comment to his code so that someone else reading his code can understand it better.

In summary, comments are simply a way of writing your own notes in the code of a computer program without it being read by the computer.

What the JVM Sees

During execution, the JVM just ignores whatever is a comment. That means that you can literally write anything. Within a comment, you can write "I love cats", and the computer will just pay no attention to it. Writing comments are simple, and there are a few different ways to do so.

Single-Line Comments

As the name implies, single line comments are used for writing comments that only last for a single line. Single line comments are used for relatively short phrases and sentences. To add a single-line comment, you simply need to add a "//" symbol before the comment. Then, you can write your comment for the rest of the line. The JVM will resume reading the code at the next line. Here is an example of a single-line comment in the Hello World program.

```
class Hello_Worldv2 {

    // This is an example of a single-line comment

    public static void main (String[] args) {

        System.out.println ("Hello World");

    }

}
```

Multi-Line Comments

The multi-line comment allows one to make a comment without having to indicate that every line is a comment. This is done using start and stop symbols. The comment is in between the start and stop symbols. The symbols are /* (Start) and */ (End). When the JVM sees "/*" it ignores all text until it sees "*/".

```
class Hello_Worldv3 {

    public static void main (String[] args) {

        /* This

        is an

        example of a

        multi-line comment
```

```
        */

        System.out.println ("Hello World");

    }

}
```

Javadoc Comments

Lastly, Javadoc comments are used for documenting information about code, such as its date, version, and description. This type of comment is different from the other two in that the computer can generate documentation based on Javadoc comments.

Javadoc is a special type of comment, from which the computer can create a document called Javadoc. Like multiline comments, Javadoc comments have a start and end character and can extend to multiple lines within the same comment.

Structure

The structure of Javadoc comments is very similar to that of multiline comments. I

Tags

Tags simply indicate a feature of the code, such as its author and version. Tags are written with an "@" symbol following the tag name (Ex: @author). The information corresponding to the tag is written after the tag. The following text indicates (in a Javadoc) that the author of the code is named Billy Bob Joe.

@author Billy Bob Joe

Certain tags are built into the Java language, such as author and version.

HTML Tags

Javadoc comments are formatted in HTML, so tags from the language can also be added to the Javadoc.

HTML is simply a language used for formatting text. This can be done by changing a text's font, color, and style. You do not need to know HTML to create a Javadoc comment. In case you do, you can add tags to the Javadoc comment and format it the way you wish. Here is an example of an HTML tag.

<b> This is an example of using an HTML tag to bold a text

Code

The Javadoc comment looks like this.

```
class Hello_Worldv4 {

    public static void main (String[] args) {

        /**

        * This is an example of a Javadoc comment.

        *

        * @author Ravit Sharma

        */

        System.out.println ("Hello World");

    }

}
```

The preceding comment produces the following Javadoc

```
This is an example of a Javadoc comment
Author:
Billy Bob Joe
```

As you can see from the program above, the comment style is like that of a multiline comment, except that it begins with "/**", not "/*" and that an "*" symbol begins the line for every line of the comment. The comment ends the same way as a multiline comment, with "*/".

How to create Javadoc

Javadoc can be produced via the IDE. Although the steps to do so vary depending on the IDE, there is generally a command that generates Javadoc. In Eclipse, there is a command called Generate Javadoc under the Project pulldown menu.

Uses

Comments are widely used by computer programmers because they are simple ways to not only describe what you are writing, but to also communicate with other people why you are typing the code that you are. When reading code, it is very easy to get lost. For that reason, comments are helpful in explaining code.

Identifiers

Identifiers are simply names given to classes, objects, variables, methods, etc. Anything to which you give a name in Java is an identifier. Their names are used to refer to the respective class, object, variable, or method. Hello_World is an identifier for the class in the Hello World program. You (the programmer) can decide the name for these identifiers. There is no limit on how long each name can be, but there are some restrictions.

Rules for Identifiers

Here is a list of rules that control the names of identifiers.

- An identifier cannot have spaces.

- An identifier can only start with letters (a-z, A-Z), currency symbols ($), or connecting punctuation characters, such as underscores (_).

- An identifier cannot start with a number.

- An identifier can only contain letters (a-z, A-Z), currency symbols ($), connecting punctuation characters, such as underscores (_), numeric letters, combining marks, digits (0-9), and non-spacing marks.

- An identifier cannot be the same as a keyword (AKA reserved words)

Examples

These are a list of sample valid identifiers:

```
$money

AReallyLongIdentifierThatJustKeepsGoingAndGoingAndGoing

I_Love_Cats

Java123

_87cats

qwertyuiopasdfghjklzxcvbnm
```

Where are Identifiers Used?

Classes

A class is a top-level block of code that holds programs. Classes are also a vital element of object-oriented programming used to create objects. Classes need to be named for a couple reasons.

1. They allow for the creation of objects (a topic further discussed in Chapter 3).

2. Since they hold programs, they allow you to tell the computer which program to run.

Here's what a class looks like.

```
class class_example {

    //CLASS CONTENT

}
```

As you can see below, class_example is the identifier for the example class shown above.

Interfaces

An interface is an advanced topic that we will get to in Chapter 4. For now, you should know that an interface is a top-level block of code containing a collection of methods. Here is what it looks like.

```
interface interface_example {

    //INTERFACE CONTENT

}
```

Again, interface_example is the identifier for the interface above.

Methods

Methods are simply a list of instructions. They are elements of classes and interfaces that perform a specific task. There are two subcategories: creating the method and calling the method.

Creating the Method

Creating the method involves listing out the instructions for the computer to perform. This is a complex process, which will be broken down more in the future. Here is what a method looks like.

```
class method_example {

    void method_example1 {

        //METHOD CONTENT

    }
```

```
void method_example2 {

    //METHOD CONTENT

}

}
```

Calling the Method

Creating a method is not useful unless those instructions are put to use. Calling a method simply means giving the set of instructions in that method to the computer to execute. In most cases, you need an object to call a method. An object is simply an instance of a class (discussed more in the next chapter). Here is what calling a method looks like.

```
OBJECT_NAME.METHOD_NAME(PARAMETERS);
```

Do not worry if the concept of methods. is still a little confusing to you. It should make more sense in the near future.

Variables

Variables are simply parts of a program that hold information.

In Java, there are many instances when we need to ask the computer to remember a piece of information, such as a number, so that later we can ask it to use that number in different tasks. Variables fulfill just this purpose. In Java, variables serve as fields of a class (and sometimes of methods too) that store information, or data. These prove to be very helpful, especially in Object-Oriented Programming because they can serve as fields of an object.

Because of variables, we don't have to keep writing the same number repeatedly in our programs. There is an easy way to ask the computer to remember these pieces of information. These are called variables.

You can think of a variable like a mailbox. The mailbox can hold something inside it, or nothing at all. The letters inside the mailbox make up the variable's value. The variable could also have nothing at all. If this variable is to hold an object, then the value of the variable is null. Null is a keyword used in Java to represent an object that has no value.

Variables can hold all sorts of information, such as letters and numbers. They are almost always used in computer programs. There are two main branches of variables: primitive types and objects. One important rule is that variables must begin with a letter. They cannot begin with a number or symbol, although numbers can be included in other parts of the name. Before we go into greater detail about them, you should know how to declare them and set their values.

Below is the general format for declaring variables. Declaring means telling the computer that they exist. This is like setting up a mailbox in front of a house. The house is an object and the mailbox is a field of the object. It may not have any letters, but it exists.

```
VARIABLE_TYPE VARIABLE_NAME;
```

Here is how you give the variables their values. This is called assignment because you are "assigning" the variable to a value.

```
VARIABLE_NAME = VARIABLE_VALUE;
```

You can

```
VARIABLE_TYPE VARIABLE_NAME = VARIABLE_VALUE;
```

Of course, in the above examples, you would have to replace VARIABLE_TYPE, VARIABLE_NAME, and VARIABLE_VALUE with their actual types, names, and values.

This format applies even in the case of objects. You will learn more about objects in the next couple of chapters.

Next, let's discuss the different types of variables in more detail.

Why Variables?

Variables are key to programming for a few reasons, including generalization, avoiding repetition, and dodging mistakes.

Generalization

Variables allow you to generalize the different values a variable can have into a single name. Methods of a class may need to refer to the class's variables. However, a class's variables may be different from object to object. Let's take an example.

Getter method for an object's serial number

The method is in the class description, but the serial number is different for each object

The getter method can use a variable for the serial number, since the variable can have different values in different objects of a class

Avoid repetition

You are writing a program to create a list of names of volunteers and send them and email.

You might come across "Mr. Wolfeschlegelsteinhausenbergerdorff" (that's a real person's name)

Without a variable

You'll have to write that twice in your program: one while creating the list, and another while sending the email

Not only is it inconvenient and tiresome to write out names twice, it also opens up the door for mistakes. (You don't want to send someone an email calling him by the wrong name.)

With a variable

You only need to make sure you spell his name correctly once: when you are assigning his name to a variable.

```
String name3 = "Mr. Wolfeschlegelsteinhausenbergerdorff";

// A VARIABLE THAT STORES THE NAME
```

Then, you can access the participant's name through the name of the variable.

```
addToList (name3);

sendEmail (name3);
```

When the email is sent, it is sent addressing "Mr. Wolfeschlegelsteinhausenbergerdorff" (the value of the variable), not name3 (the name of the variable).

Capturing Unknown Values

Sometimes, programmers need to deal with values they don't know while programming. For example, what if they have to refer to user input multiple times throughout the program? Certain values may remain constant each time a program is run. User input, however, won't be. To do this, the programmer can create a variable that can hold the unknown value.

```
VARIABLE_TYPE user_input = USER_INPUT_VALUE;
```

Dodge mistakes

While typing, it is not uncommon to misspell a word. Using variables reduces the chances of you making an error, and makes your life much easier if you do mess up.

For example, you may be writing a program preparing for a party for 17 people and want to order one slice of cake for each person you invite.

```
invitePeople (17);

//INVITES 17 PEOPLE

orderCakeSlices (17);

//ORDERS 17 CAKE SLICES
```

Sometimes, you might make a mistake while typing and press "16" instead of "17". Instead of ordering 17 cake slices, you write the code to order 16 slices.

```
orderCakeSlices (16);
```

```
//ORDERS 16 CAKE SLICES
```

Now you have 17 people you invited to the party, but only 16 slices of cake. That's a problem.

You can change this with variables.

```
int Invite_Count = 17;

//CREATES A VARIABLE TO STORE THE VALUE

invitePeople (Invite_Count);

orderCakeSlices (Invite_Count);
```

This invites 17 people to the party and orders 17 slices of cake. With variables, you only need to make sure that the number of people you want to invite is right: that is where you assign the variable. Everywhere else, you can be sure that the number is right; it must be.

If you misspell the variable name, the compiler will not understand what you mean and throw an error (unless you misspell it such that it changes the meaning of the code).

Variables greatly reduce the risk for error.

Scope

Variables have something called scope, which simply refers to the area where variables live. In simpler terms, this means the region where variables are visible. If a line of code exists within a class, it is within the class's scope. If it exists inside a method, it is within the method's scope, and is thus visible. A variable is visible anywhere within its scope.

Below are two types of scope that variables exist within.

Instance Variables

An instance variable is simply a type of variable that belongs to an object. In other words, this is essentially a variable of a class declared inside or outside a method. Here is an example of a program with two instance variables.

```
class instance_variables {

    VARIABLE_TYPE instance1 = VARIABLE_VALUE;

    void method1 () {}

    VARIABLE_TYPE instance2 = VARIABLE_VALUE;

}
```

Keep in mind that the code above will not work, as VARIABLE_TYPE and VARIABLE_VALUE will have to be replaced with the type of variable and the value of the variable, respectively.

Instance variables can be accessed from anywhere within the class, since their scope is the class itself.

Method-Local Variables

Method-Local variables are variables declared and used within methods. Although the primary purpose of methods is to execute a series of tasks, variables are also sometimes useful. Their scope is the method in which they are declared. Here is an example.

```
class method-local_variables {

    void method1 () {

        VARIABLE_TYPE method-local1 = VARIABLE_VALUE;

        VARIABLE_TYPE method-local2 = VARIABLE_VALUE2

    }

}
```

Since the scope of these two variables is the method, they are not visible anywhere outside the method, including other methods. As a result, other methods can contain

Declaration

Declaring a variable is used to tell the computer that there is a variable that exists. Declaring a variable as a field of the class gives it a default value, which is discussed later on. Going back to our old analogy of the mailbox, declaring a variable is like installing a mailbox in front of somebody's house.

```
VARIABLE_TYPE VARIABLE_NAME;
```

Assignment

Assignment means giving a variable a value. Different values exist for different types of variables, as we will see soon. A variable can be assigned even if the variable already has an existing value, giving a variable a new value. This is how variables are assigned in Java.

```
VARIABLE_NAME = VARIABLE_VALUE;
```

Assigning one variable to another

It is also possible to assign one variable to another, as shown below.

```
VARIABLE VAR_1 = VARIABLE_VALUE;

VARIABLE VAR_2 = VAR_1;
```

As you can see, one variable was assigned to the name of another variable. What does this do? This doesn't make a copy of the value in VAR_1 and place it in VAR_2. Instead, it creates two names for the same value. It is like a nickname. Let's say there is a boy named Robert whose nickname is Bob. Robert and Bob aren't two different people; they are just two different names for the same person. If the value of the variable were changed, then it changes for both values. If Robert gets a candy, then Bob also gets a candy. The action above has a similar effect.

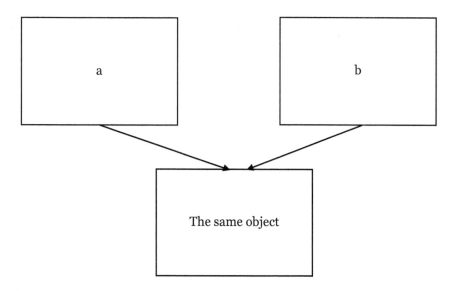

Default Values for Variables

It is not required to assign a primitive type to a value immediately when it is declared. In case a

Variable	Default Value
boolean	false
char	0
int	0
short	0

byte	0
long	0
float	0.0
double	0.0
object	null

Primitive Types

A primitive type is a category of variables that hold certain types of values. Different primitive types exist for different kinds of values. Examples of values include numbers, strings, and characters.

Integers

Integers are types of variables that hold whole numbers. Examples of whole numbers are 0, 3, -49, 24, and -1224. Unlike how we write numbers in real life, we do not add commas to numbers when coding. Instead of 6,428 we write 6428. However, there is a limit to how large and how small these numbers can be. An integer in Java is a whole number, positive or negative, between -2147483648 and 2147483647. The reason for this size constraint has to do with the way data is stored in computer.

To declare an integer in Java, we use the word "int" followed by the variable name. Remember that all statements, like this one, must end with a semicolon.

A sample declaration and assignment of an integer is as follows.

```
int i;

i = 3;
```

Of course, this variable can have any name and any value. Here is another sample declaration and assignment.

```
int another_int;

another_int = 561431;
```

As was mentioned before, the declaration and assignment can even be combined.

```
int one_more_int = 561431;
```

double

double is another primitive type that has to do with numbers. More specifically, it stores decimal points instead of whole numbers. Examples of decimal points include 2.42, 15.343, -421.3, and 3.0.

To declare a double, use the keyword "double", followed by the name of your variable. To assign the variable, use the "=" symbol, and then the number to which you want to assign your variable.

```
double d;

d = 23.3;

double another_double = 7.42421;
```

float

float is another primitive type like double. The only difference is the range of the two. To learn more about this, visit the online API specification of Oracle. Here is what a float primitive type looks like.

```
float f;

f = 678.56;

float another_float = 45.7849;
```

long

long is another primitive type that holds whole numbers can hold whole numbers, like integers. The difference is their range. longs have a much larger capacity than do ints. They can hold any number from -9,223,372,036,854,775,808 to 9,223,372,036,854,775,807.

Bytes, Shorts and Short Casting

The next two variables, bytes and shorts, are also variables that hold whole numbers, but they are categorized separately because their range is smaller than the range of integers. If we were to declare them like integers, there would be a type mismatch since the computer assumes that all whole numbers are integers, unless it is provided with other information. To tell the computer that the numbers are indeed bytes and shorts, and not integers, we need to do something called short casting. That means that we are going to tell the computer that these numbers are not integers (like the computer assumes), but bytes and shorts. We can short cast by prefixing the value of the variable with the name of the variable in parentheses, as you will see in the following declaration and assignment. This is required, because otherwise, the computer assumes that these numbers are integers.

```
byte b = (byte) 34;

short s = (short) 232;
```

The range of bytes is from -128 to 127, and the range of shorts is from -32,768 to 32,767.

Strings

Strings are types of variables that hold series of symbols, letters, and white spaces (pressing the space bar or the tab button on your keyboard). In Java, it is always important to use quotation marks around the text we assign to a string, or text that is used in any other action. To declare a string in Java, we use the word "String" followed by the name of the variable. An example of a string declaration and assignment is as follows.

```
String anything;

anything = "RANDOM";
```

The two can be combined.

```
String another_string = "another random string";
```

Characters

Characters are like strings, except that they hold only one letter, number or symbol. Rather than being surrounded by quotation marks they are surrounded by single quotes. To declare a character in Java, we need to write "char" followed by the variable name.

```
char c;

c = 'D';
```

Boolean

Boolean values are simply true or false. They are either set to "true" by the programmer if they are true, or they are set to "false" if they are false. There are only two options available for this type of variable, which makes it unique. Here is an example of a boolean.

```
boolean true_or_false = true;
```

Arrays

An array is something that holds a group of primitive types and objects. Think of a store. A store arranges their products using aisles. Each aisle has a different category. For example, one aisle may have food products, while the other may have toys. Different aisles hold a different type of product.

Arrays are like

Arrays are simply a group of variables or objects. They are objects themselves that can hold up to a specified number of items in it. You can think of arrays like a room full of things, where each room can hold one type of thing. One room might hold books; another might hold old pictures; another might hold a collection of DVDs.

The room is the array, and the boxes are the elements of the array.

Dimension

Think of dimension like this. You have a straight line. On this straight line, a point can only go back and forth. Now let's add another dimension. Turn it into a square. Now you can not only go back and forth, but also side to side. If we add yet another dimension and turn that into a cube, we can go back and forth, side to side, and up and down. Therefore, a line has one dimension, a square has two dimensions, and a cube has three dimensions. That's how dimension works.

Arrays also have dimensions. However, unlike in the real world, arrays can have infinitely many dimensions (if the computer has enough memory).

Declaration

The declaration part of arrays is like the declaration of variables. The declaration of a single-dimension array goes like this.

```
VARIABLE_TYPE [] ARRAY_NAME;
```

If we were to create a multidimensional array, we would set the number of open and close brackets to the number of dimensions we want to add. For example, here is a declaration of a three-dimensional array.

```
VARIABLE_TYPE [][][] ARRAY_NAME;
```

Assignment

In the assignment of an array, we include the keyword "new" (to indicate that a new object is being created), as well as the size of the dimensions. However, we do not yet include the contents of the array. An assignment of a one-dimensional array looks like this.

```
ARRAY_NAME = new VARIABLE_TYPE[DIMENSION_SIZE];
```

The dimension size indicates how large you want the array to be for a single dimension. The same process is repeated with multiple dimensions as follows.

```
ARRAY_NAME = new
VARIABLE_TYPE[DIMENSION_SIZE1][DIMENSION_SIZE2][DIMENSION_SIZE
3];
```

Filling Up the Array

An array holds items, so we have to find a way to fill it with them. The way we do this is to indicate which item we want to fill up, and assign it to the appropriate value. Below is the syntax for doing so.

```
ARRAY_NAME[INDEX] = VALUE;
```

This is also applied to multidimensional arrays.

```
ARRAY_NAME[INDEX1][INDEX2] = VALUE;
```

This can get complicated sometimes, so to help simplify this in your mind, you can think of arrays as a chart full of values, and to insert a value in the array, we have to locate where the box is and put the correct value. However, there is an important rule that all programmers should be aware of. When you assign an array, you indicate how many items each dimension can hold. However, when giving each slot a value, the count starts from 0, not 1. As a result, we could assign an array: "numbers = new int[2];", but not be able to execute the following: "numbers[2] = 231;". There are two integers in the array, but since they start from 0, the two slots include "numbers[0]" and "numbers[1]".

Print Commands

There are two commands telling the computer to print something to the console. Those are:

```
System.out.print ("TEXT");
```

```
System.out.println ("TEXT");
```

(The former was used in our "Hello World" program). These two commands are very similar, but there is one key difference. The first command tells the computer to just print whatever is within the parentheses. The second command tells the computer to print what is within the parentheses and move to the next line (notice the "ln" before the parentheses). This is useful if one is planning to print more information. For example, if there were a program telling the computer to print a series of multidigit numbers. If the print command were used, then it would be hard to tell when one number ends and the next starts (computers don't add spaces before or after numbers by themselves)

```
System.out.print ("54");

System.out.print ("9");
```

prints 549, not 54 9. Anyway, if we used the println command, then the numbers would be separated by a new line, making it easy to spot the different numbers.

```
System.out.println ("54");

System.out.println ("9");
```

The code above should produce the following output.

```
54

9
```

toString() method

The two print commands described above don't only print strings. They also print much more. Strings are able to print virtually any field, variable, or value in a program, including objects and primitive types. System.out.print () and System.out.println (); are two methods. Recall that methods are simply instructions for the computer. These descriptions of these methods belong to the class java.lang.System, and show the computer what to do when the command is called. In short, they tell the computer how to print what is in the parameters, or the parentheses – (). These descriptions also allow the programmer to print values other than strings, such as primitive types and objects. To do this, simply place an identifer or value of a variable inside the parameter and run the program. Let's look at an example.

2 Foundation

```
class print_cmd {

    public static void main (String [] args) {

        //--- PRIMITIVE TYPES ---


        //PRINT COMMAND USING A VALUE


        //PRINTING AN INTEGER

        System.out.println (2);

        //PRINTING A BOOLEAN

        System.out.println (true);

        //PRINTING A CHAR

        System.out.println ('c');

        //PRINTING A STRING

        System.out.println ("string");


        // PRINT COMMAND USING AN IDENTIFIER


        int i = 2;

        boolean b = true;

        char c = 'c';

        String s = "string";


        //PRINTING AN INTEGER

        System.out.println (i);
```

```
//PRINTING A BOOLEAN

System.out.println (b);

//PRINTING A CHAR

System.out.println (c);

//PRINTING A STRING

System.out.println (s);


//--- OBJECTS ---


//PRINT COMMAND USING A VALUE


System.out.println (new Object ());


//PRINT COMMAND USING AN IDENTIFIER


Object o = new Object ();
System.out.println (o);
/*Printing an object does not simply print the
object's name to the console. Instead, it prints a
string representation of that object, which contains
the class of the object and a hexadecimal hash code
(simply a series of letters and numbers) that is
different for each object. Here is an example of
what you might see when you call the print command
```

```
        on an object. java.lang.Object@36aa7bc2*/

    }

}
```

Here is the output:

```
2

true

c

string

2

true

c

string

java.lang.Object@1175e2db

java.lang.Object@36aa7bc2
```

Operators

As you may recall from Chapter 1, operations are commands given to the computer. And operators are characters that signify actions. That is a general definition, and it is brief because there are many different operators that do different things. This section will only cover what are the most important operators in my opinion. To simplify operators, let us break them down into two major categories: numerical operators and logical operators.

Numerical operators are like the operators you have learned about in math. Addition, subtraction, multiplication, and division are all examples of numerical operators. However, these are not the only kinds of operators. In Java, there is another branch of operators called logical operators. Unlike numerical operators, logical operators do not have to do with making calculations. Instead, they deal with deal with mathematical calculations, while logical operators cover pretty much everything else.

Boolean Operators

Boolean Operators get their name because they compare two values. Like the assignment operator, these operators require there to be a value both on the left and on the right of the operator. UnlikeThese provide boolean values, so they can be used as a substitute for true or false values in assignments and conditions. Some examples of relational operators include ==, >, <, >=, <=, and !. The following table should help you understand these operators better.

Operator	Function
==	True if both values on either side of the operator are equal
>	True if value on the left is greater than value on the right; can only be used with numerical values
<	True if value on the right is greater than value on the left; can only be used with numerical values
>=	True if value on the left is greater than or equal to value on the right; can only be used with numerical values
<=	True if value on the right is greater than or equal to value on the

	left; can only be used with numerical values
!	Used before other operators, provides opposite of what the value would have been if it wasn't present[2]

As I stated earlier, these operators can be used as boolean values. For example, I can assign a boolean variable like the following.

```
boolean example = 1 == 1;
```

The "!" symbol can be used to provide the opposite value. True values become false, and false values become true. For example, if we were to use "1 != 1" in the above example, the value would have been false.

Assignment Operator

The assignment operator is used to place a value inside a variable. The operator is simply an equal sign, and is used in the assignments of variables. The variable goes on the left-hand side, and the value goes on the right-hand side.

---

[2] This operator is used in conjunction with other relational operators to reverse their value. Except for == (which becomes !=), all new operators are formed by placing ! before the operator.

We have already seen examples of assignment operators when we worked with variables. They are operators that are used to set values of not only variables, but also objects, the main actors in Object Oriented Programming. The only assignment operator is the "=" symbol. The name of the variable or object to which we want to assign another value is on the left-hand side of the equal sign, and the value which we want to assign it is on the right-hand side of the equal sign as you will see in the following example.

```
FIELD_NAME = FIELD_VALUE;
```

This operator should seem familiar from the section on variables. Assignment operators provide the basis for programming in Java.

Numerical Operators

Numerical operators are operators related to numbers and their interactions. There are two major types of numerical operators: arithmetic, and increment and decrement operators.

Arithmetic Operators

Arithmetic Operators are operators that deal with basic operations. Specifically, they cover addition, subtraction, multiplication, division, and remainder. You have probably learned about most of these. Addition involves finding the sum of two numerical values, subtraction involves finding the difference of two numerical values, multiplication involves finding the product of two numerical values, and division involves finding the quotient of two numerical values. The remainder operator divides two numbers and finds and returns the remainder. The symbols for the operators described above are as follows.

Operator	Function

+	Adds two numbers
-	Subtracts two numbers
*	Multiplies two numbers
/	Divides two numbers
%	Performs Modulus on two numbers
()	Indicates that the operation within them is to be performed first

Here is an example of an operator put to use.

```
class operator_example {
    public static void main (String[] args) {
        int i = ((3 + 3)/2)%2;
        System.out.println(i);
        //i is evaluated and then printed
    }
}
```

The output of this program should be 1.

Increment and Decrement Operators

++ and -- are used to increment and decrement numbers respectively. Increment means to increase the value by a fixed amount, and decrement means to decrease the value by a fixed amount, and are mostly used in assignments or by themselves. They are used before or after a number, but they have slightly different effects if used either way in assignments. In this case, the numbers are incremented or decremented by one. For example, if we set the value of an integer (let's say i) to one, and then use the "++" operator on it in the statement "i++;", its new value will be two. They can also be used in assignments

```
int i = 0;

int j = 0;

i = ++j;
```

This increments "j", and then sets "i" to the value of "j", which is 1 after it is incremented. However, we can switch around the steps, like in the following code.

```
int i = 0;

int j = 0;

i = j++;
```

Now, "i" is set to the value of "j", and then "j" is incremented. As opposed to the first example in which "i" was 1, "i" is now 0.

There is a new way of assigning the values of numerical variables. They combine both the assignment operator and the arithmetic operators. They literally consist of a numerical operator followed without a space by an equal sign.

```
int i = 0;

int j = 1;

i += j;
```

This has an effect equal to "i = i + j;". This may not make sense in mathematics, but in Java, this simply states that the new value of "i" is equal to the old value of "i" plus the value of "j". Similarly, this style of writing can be used with "-=", "*=", "/=", and "%=".

Control Statements

"If" Statements

"If" statements perform a statement if a certain condition is true. A condition is a statement of boolean value that can be determined to be either true or false. This is usually used if the programmer is uncertain whether the condition will be satisfied or not. For example, the condition could check whether the time is past noon, and only then change the time to p.m. "If" statements always use boolean operators, which is why you should always refer back to the boolean operators in the previous section. The code for "If" statements is as follows.

```
if (CONDITION) {

    // if the condition above turns out to be true, then

    // execute this code

}
```

Here is an example of an "If" statement with a valid condition.

```
if (1 == 1) {

    // Since the condition above is true, the code within

    // the scope of this "If" Statement will be executed.

    System.out.println("One is equal to one");

}
```

Sometimes, the condition is false, so the code within the scope is not executed, as we will see in the next example.

```
if (1 == 2) {

    // Since the condition above is false, the

    // following code will not be executed.

    System.out.println("One is equal to two");

}
```

"Else If" Statements

"Else If" statements are identical to "If" statements, except that the condition of the "Else If" statement is only checked by the program if the condition of the previous "If" Statement is false. To reiterate: code within the scope of in "Else If" statement is only executed if both the condition in the "If" statement is incorrect and the "Else" condition is valid. Let's look at an example.

```
if (1 == 2) {

    // Once again, the following code will not be

    // executed because the condition above is false

    System.out.println("One is equal to two.");

}

else if (1 == 1) {

    // Since the condition above is valid, and the

    // condition in the "If" statement is invalid, the

    // following code will be executed

    System.out.println("One is equal to one");

}
```

To clarify issues that come up in coding, "Else If" statements have to directly follow "If" or other "Else If" statements. You cannot write an "If" statement, then declare a variable, and then write an "Else If" statements. Unlike "If" statements, "Else If" statements cannot be nested by themselves; they depend on being around another "If" statement.

"Else" Statements

"Else" statements are an addition to "If" and "Else If" statements. The else portion also contains a scope that contains code that is only executed if the conditions in the "If" and "Else If" statements are determined to be false. This is used after an "If" or after an "Else If" statement. However, it does not contain a condition, and depends on the validity (correctness) of the condition in the "If" and "Else If" statement. The format for the code is as follows.

```
if (CONDITION) {

    // if the condition is true, execute this code

}

else if (CONDITION) {

    // if the condition of the if statement is not

    // satisfied and the above condition is, then this

    // code is to be executed

}

else {

    // if the condition of both if and if else

    // statements were not true, execute this code

}
```

Here is an example of an "If Else" statement

```
if (4 * 2 == 7)

{
```

57

```
// This will never happen because four times two

// is equal to eight, not seven

System.out.println ("Four times two is equal to seven.");

}

else {

    // This will happen because the original if

    // statement was not satisfied

    // 4 times 2 is not equal to seven

    System.out.println ("Four times two is not equal to
seven.");

}
```

"Else" statements only exist directly after an "Else If" or an "If" statement. However, there can be only one "Else" statement for an "If" statement. Once you write an "Else" statement, you cannot write any more "Else" statements for the original "If" statement.

"Switch" Statements

Switch statements are a method of matching a particular variable to one of several cases provided. If the value of the variable matches one of the cases provided in the switch statement, then the code for that case and the rest of the succeeding cases is executed. There are a few keywords used in a switch statement: switch, case, and default.

The switch statement is often used when the value being matched is unknown. It is compared to options, and if there is a match, the code is executed. If not

Structure

Here is the structure of a switch statement.

2 Foundation

```
switch (value) {

    case case1:

        //Code for case 1

    case case2:

        //Code for case 2

}
```

// Note that the type of case1 and case2 have to match the

// case of value to prevent the compiler from throwing an

// error

As you can see above, the switch keyword is followed by a parameter for a variable as well as brackets containing the cases. A colon follows each case. The JVM identifies the value of the variable and matches it to the value after each case keyword. The two must be the same type (a boolean cannot be matched to an int). However, the value and the cases to which it is matched can be variables. In the above, example, "value", "case1", and "case2" can be identifiers for variables. In that case, the compiler matches the value of those variables. If the values of the two values/variables are the same, all the code after the colon for that case keyword is executed, until the end of the switch statement (or until something called a break statement). Even code for other cases is executed.

Let's look at an example involving the switch statement. There is an integer set to 3. Different cases are matched to that integer.

```
class Switch_Example {

    public static void main (String [] args) {

        int i = 3;

        switch (i) {

            case 1:

                // NO MATCH
```

```
        System.out.println ("1");

    case 2:

        // NO MATCH

        System.out.println ("2");

    case 3:

        // MATCH! CODE EXECUTION STARTS

        System.out.println ("3");

    case 4:

        // NO MATCH! CODE EXECUTION CONTINUES

        System.out.println ("4");

    case 5:

        // NO MATCH! CODE EXECUTION CONTINUES

        System.out.println ("5");

    }

  }

}
```

The output should be the following:

3

4

5

Break statement

The break statement can be used to interrupt the execution of a switch statement. If a match is found, execution of the code does not stop until the end. However, if a break statement is used, execution of the switch statement stops, and code resumes execution after the switch statement.

2 Foundation

The break statement is just the keyword "break" followed by a semicolon. Here's an example of a switch statement with a break.

```
class Switch_Break_Example {

    public static void main (String [] args) {

        int i = 3;

        switch (i) {

            case 1:

                // NO MATCH

                System.out.println ("1");

                //BREAK STATEMENT NOT EXECUTED

                break;

            case 2:

                // NO MATCH

                System.out.println ("2");

                break;

            case 3:

                // MATCH! CODE EXECUTION STARTS

                System.out.println ("3");

                break;

                // BREAK! CODE EXECUTION STOPS

            case 4:

                // NO MATCH

                System.out.println ("4");

                break;

            case 5:
```

```
// NO MATCH

System.out.println ("5");

break;

            }

      }

}
```

The output should be the following:

3

Loops

Loops are simply statements that repeat themselves. They can repeat themselves as long as a condition is satisfied. Loops in Java have three parts that keep the loop going for however long you want them to. They are initialization, increment, and condition.

In initialization, a field, usually an integer, is prepared for repetition. This involves declaring and assigning a variable. If you are using an already declared variable, simply assign it. If you do not want to change its value, simply leave the field blank. After initialization, the field is checked to ensure that it meets the condition through logical operators. If it doesn't, the loop is exited; else, it repeats. In traditional loops, that field is incremented every repetition after the condition is checked. This is done using numerical operators, which were discussed earlier. If the initialized field is an integer, it is usually added or subtracted.

"For" Loops

For loops have a standard format that you must follow to produce a working loop. You don't have to program them to follow it properly; just substitute the capitalized words with their values with the rest of the code just as it is written, and you will get the proper output.

2 Foundation

```
for (INITIALIZATION; CONDITION CHECKING; INCREMENT)

{

CODE THAT IS TO BE REPEATED UNTIL THE CONDITION

IS FALSE

}
```

Here are the statements that for loops go through:

1. Initialization (only once)

2. Loop – until condition is false

    a. Condition Checking

    b. Code to repeat

    c. Increment

The order of these sections in execution is: initialization, condition checking, code, and lastly increment. This sequence repeats until the condition is false. Here is an example of a "For" loop that prints out all the numbers from 0 to 10.

```
for (int i = 0; i < 10;i++)

{

    System.out.println(i);

}
```

This is a common example of a "For" loop. It starts off by declaring an integer and setting it to 0, then checks that it is less than or equal to 10, prints out the integer using the "System.out.println" command (from Chapter 2), adds one to itself (making it one), and again checks the condition, therefore starting the whole process all over again. This repeats until the integer's value increments to 10. The condition is checked, and is false because 10 is not less than 10. Since the condition is false, the loop is exited, with all numbers from 0 to 9 printed.

It is also possible to create a loop that runs forever. Simply create a condition that is always true (such as 1 == 1), and run the program. Another way to do this is to leave the condition blank, so that the loop never stops. Alternatively, all sections except the code can be left blank.

```
for (  ;   ;   ) {

CODE THAT IS TO BE REPEATED FOREVER

}
```

Foreach Loops

Foreach loops are special loops that involve iterating through an array. This allows you to perform an action to each element of the array. For example, let's say that you want to add 1 to each integer in an array. That would be a good place to use the foreach loop.

A foreach loop is like a regular for loop in that it uses the for keyword. The only difference is that there are only two parameters: the element that represents the parts of the array, and the array itself. By the way, you can give any name to the element taken in as the parameter of the loop, and refer to that within the block. Each element of the array is not named, so you can give it a name you choose. However, you must use the same name for the array through which you are iterating. These two are separated by a colon (:). This loop simply tells the JVM to go through elements of the array and for each element, execute the statements inside the block. Here's what it looks like:

```
for (Element_Type Element_Name : Array_Name) {

    //Statements go here and are executed for every element in
the array

    //Actions can be performed on Element_Name

}
```

Note that Array_Name must be declared and assigned before the foreach loop.

Here's a simple example that adds 1 to each integer in an array of integer.

```
int [] numbers = new int [3];

numbers [0] = 0;

numbers [1] = 1;

numbers [2] = 2;

for (int i : numbers []) {

    i += 1;

}
```

After the program is run, then the values of numbers [0], numbers [1], and numbers [2] should be 1, 2, and 3 respectively.

"While" Loops

A "While" loop is another type of loop. Again, the computer understands what to do when it reads the word "while"; all you have to do is replace the capitalized words with their actual code.

```
INITIALIZATION

while (CONDITION) {

    CODE

    INCREMENT

}
```

As you can see, a "While" loop is like a "For" loop in that they both have parentheses and a scope. However, in the while loop, initialization is outside the loop, condition is within the parentheses of the condition, and the code and increment are within the scope of the loop. Now let's see how we can write numbers from 0 to 10 using a while loop.

```
int i = 0;

while (i <= 10) {

    System.out.println(i);
```

```
    i++;

}
```

A while loop works in very much the same way as a for loop, although there are some situations where one may be preferable over another.

"Do While"

Lastly, "Do While" is a slightly different approach to create a loop. The major difference between this and just a plain "While" loop is that the code within the scope is executed before the condition is checked. That means that the code is executed at least once whether the condition is true or not. The syntax for "Do While" loops is as follows.

```
DECLARATION

do {

    CODE

    INCREMENT

}

while (CONDITION);
```

As you can see, the syntax is identical except that the scope of the loop occurs before the "while" with a do before the scope. Again, there are situations where this is beneficial over other loops, and is included to present to you the wide variety of options available in Java.

```
class Do_While {

    public static void main (String [] args) {

        do {

            System.out.println ("Executed");

        }

        while (1 == 0);
```

```
        }

}
```

As you can see above, the code of the loop is executed once before the condition is checked. Even the condition is always false, Executed is printed once. As a result, this is the output of the program:

```
Executed
```

Here is another example of a do while loop that prints numbers 0 to 10.

```
int i = 0;

do {

    System.out.println (i);

    i++;

}

while (i < 10)
```

Here is the output of this program.

```
0

1

2

3

4

5

6

7

8

9
```

Break statement

"break" is a keyword used to exit a loop or switch. You have already seen "break" as used in a switch. They can also be used to exit a "while" or "for" loop and go to the statement after the loop, if any. "break" is useful when you want the loop to continue to repeat in a special case. Sometimes, this keyword can act as a second condition, along with the "if" statement. Let's look at an example. You may be searching an array of Strings for the element "cat". Once you find that string, you print "true" to the console. After that, there is no need to keep looking through the array, as you have already located that string.

```java
class Loop_Break_Example {

    public static void main (String [] args) {

        String [] animals = {"dog", "bear", "cat", "giraffe"};


        for (String animal: animals) {

            if (animal == "cat") {

                System.out.println("true");

                break;

                // Exits the loop

            }

            else {

                System.out.println("false");

            }

        }

        /*After the loop is exited, the JVM starts executing
code again here*/

    }
```

```
}
```

As you can see in the code above, "cat" is the third element of the array. The loop iterates a total ot three times, two times before a match is made. As a result, the output for this program should be as follows.

```
false

false

true
```

Keywords

Keywords are words in the Java language that are used for a specific purpose. Keywords are reserved words and cannot be used as the names of identifiers. Some keywords with which you should already be familiar include "class", "int", "if", and more. In short, pretty much any code that is not an identifier or a comment is a keyword. Let's look at an example. All the highlighted words in the following program are keywords.

```
public class Keywords_Example {

    public static void main (String [] args) {

        // CODE

    }

}
```

Final

Final is a keyword in Java used in variables, methods, and classes. This keyword has different meanings when used on each of these, but in short, it used to prevent something from being changed.

Final is a keyword used to modify fields of a class. If a field in a class is final, then its value cannot be changed. A field that is final cannot be changed, and is also known as immutable.

The output of the following

```
int i = 0;

System.out.println(i);

i = 1;

System.out.println(i);
```

would be

0

1

However, if we add the final keyword to the beginning of the declaration, the variable's value cannot be changed.

```
final int i = 0;

System.out.println(i);

i = 1;

//Reassigning the value of i is not allowed

//The compiler will throw an error

System.out.println(i);
```

These statements cannot be executed as there is an error in the program: the value of the final variable cannot be reassigned.

Variables

"Final" is a keyword prefixed to variables that prevents their values can be changed. Traditionally, however, their values can be changed. Let's look at an example.

```
int i = 0;
```

```
i = 1;
```

This statement simply assigns a variable (i) to a value, and then changes that value. This is allowed. However, if the variable (i) is prefixed with the "final" keyword, then its value cannot be changed.

```
final i = 0;
```

```
i = 1;
```

When these statements are executed, the JVM will complain (i.e. throw an error) because once you put a value in the box of a variable, that value cannot change (it is final).

Method

If a method is final, then it cannot be overridden by a subclass. All methods except constructors can be declared final (a final can only be declared, public, private, or protected). It is useful to declare a method final if its implementation should never be changed. There are many examples of this in the Object class, as there are methods that should not be changed.

Here is what a final method looks like.

```
public final void final_method () {


}
```

The main method can also be declared final so that the subclasses are not able to change the implementation.

Class

A final class is one whose subclass cannot be declared. All its contents are final, and are not subject to change. If a class is labeled final, then you cannot declare a subclass of it. Here is what a final class looks like.

```
final class final_class {
```

}

Static

Static is a keyword that can modify the fields and methods of a class. If a field or method is static, that means it only occurs once-per-class. Non-static fields may have different values for their fields for different objects. One lamp object might be turned on, while the other might be turned off.

Static Fields

What if there are certain characteristics that only belong to the class. The lamp class may need to have a field called "count" to keep track of how many lamps exist within the program. The number is the same for all lamp objects. Regardless of the lamp object, the number of lamps in existence does not change. count then might as well be static, meaning that it belongs to the class. There is only one value of count, which is shared by all objects. If one object changes count, then its value changes for all the other lamp objects as well. It is a shared field.

Since static fields are shared by all objects of the class, they can be accessed through either classes or objects. Since they do not belong to an object, it is recommended that they are accessed through the class, as shown below (CLASS_NAME is the name of the class and STATIC_FIELD is the static field).

```
CLASS_NAME.STATIC_FIELD
```

Within the same class, a static field can either be referenced using just the name of the static field, or in the way shown above.

Static Methods

Static methods are exactly what they sound like; they are methods that exist once per class. Like static fields, these belong not to the object, but to the class. Static methods can be called from an object, since all objects share this method, but it is recommended to reference this through the class.

Creating a Pattern Program

Let's put what we have learned to use. Here is a tutorial to create a pattern that produces all the even numbers from 0 to 10. We will do this using a main method in a class. That method will use a for loop with an integer to print the numbers to the console. Let's get to the code.

```
public class pattern {

    public static void main (String [] args) {

        for (int i = 0; i <= 10; i = i + 2) {

            System.out.println (i);

        }

    }

}
```

As you can see in the program above, we have an integer that is set to the value of 0, and is increased by two every repetition of the for loop as long as that integer is under 10. Within that loop, the integer is printed. Since the integer is being incremented by 2 every repetition, and it is starting from 0, the integer's value will be 0, then 2, 4, 6, 8, and 10. Every time this happens, its value is printed to the console. At the end of the program, we see that the pattern has been printed to the console.

0

2

4

6

8

10

Questions

Multiple Choice

1. Which keyword is used to make a field or method once-per-class?

    a. final

    b. void

    c. return

    d. static

2. Which control statement is best to use when matching a value to one of several options?

    a. for loop

    b. if statement

    c. switch statement

    d. do while loop

3. Which of the following is a boolean operator?

    a. =

    b. %

    c. <=

    d. *

4. Which keyword is used to exit a loop or switch statement?

    a. break

    b. stop

    c. exit

    d. return

5. Which keyword is used to exit a method?

    a. break

    b. stop

    c. exit

    d. return

6. What is the numerical operator used to multiply two numbers?

    a. %

    b. #

    c. X

    d. *

7. Which keyword is a modifier for classes, fields, and methods, to prevent their contents from being changed?

    a. static

    b. void

    c. final

    d. nochange

8. What loop is used to go through elements of an array?

a. do while

b. for

c. while

d. for each

True/False

T F		A class can be declared final.
T F		The break keyword is used to stop execution of a method.
T F		Relational operators are used to provide a boolean value.
T F		The double and float primitive types hold whole numbers only.
T F		The primitive type int can only store positive numbers.

Free Response

1. Explain the two types of relational operators, and their functions. Be sure to include examples for each.

2. What are loops? Explain the three elements of loops. Explain the for, foreach, while, and do while loops with an example.

3. Explain the "If", "Else If", and "Else" control statement with an example.

4. Explain the switch statement with an example.

5. Explain the advantages of using variables.

6. Write a program that uses a loop to print the string "I love Java." ten times.

3 OBJECT-ORIENTED PROGRAMMING

In this chapter, we will learn the basics of Object-Oriented Programming (abbreviated as OOP). This is an approach to computer programming that involves the creation and interaction of things with state and behavior, called objects.

Objects

What is an object?

What do you imagine when you think of an object? It's a vague term, right? Objects in computer programming are not all that different from objects in real life. In computer science, an object has two components: state and behavior.

State and Behavior

You can ask yourself two questions to describe an object: "What is it like?" and "What can it do?" The answers of these two questions tell you the state and behavior of an object, respectively.

The state of an object is simply the characteristics that make it up. For example, a fan can either be on or off. The condition of it being on or off describes its state. A car can have different colors. Its color describes its state. Objects have several characteristics that make up its state. A car doesn't just have color. It also has a serial number, engine type, tire pressure, etc. Altogether, these features make up its state.

Behavior consists of what objects can do. A car can do several things such as accelerate, brake, steer, turn on headlights, turn on wipers, etc. (of course not by itself, but with a driver).

State describes an object (what it looks like, what color it is, how much it weighs). Behavior describes what an object does, such as beeping (in the case of a watch), turning on (in the case of a light bulb), and dispensing snacks (in the case of a vending machine).

Software Objects vs. Objects in Real Life

Objects in real life are tangible, i.e. they can be touched, felt, seen etc. Software is used to model real life objects and must possess a way to correctly describe their state and behavior. The main difference between real life objects and software objects is that the latter aren't tangible. You cannot touch them. They have states and behaviors, but they cannot be seen because they are abstracted models. They exist only in the program, much like how dreams only exist within your imagination. However, you can make objects come to life by asking the computer to describe them. For example, you can the computer to tell you if the lamp object is on or off. If it is off, you can ask the computer to turn it on and vice versa.

Objects can even interact with each other. For example, a remote can tell the TV to turn on. The remote is not part of the TV, but it has the capability to communicate with the TV and tell it to turn on.

Objects come from Classes

To create an object in computer science, we first must create a class. A class is simply a description of an object. For example, the class of a car may have fields such as color, size, model, type, dealer, and Serial Number. The fields of an object simply make up its data, and are used to describe is state. A car having color is a field, but a specific car being red is a certain object's state. Behaviors are added to the class so that objects come equipped with all the features of the class. When an object is created from that class, it comes with all the desired contents. The process of creating an object from a class is called instantiation.

You can think of a class like a prototype or blueprint for the object. It is not the actual object, but it contains all the information required to make the object, including the fields and methods. That way, when the object is created, the fields can be changed to suit the object, and different methods can be called (and sometimes even changed via anonymous classes, Chapter 9).

Creating an object from a class is like filling out an empty form, like one from a dentist appointment. An empty form has fields, such as name, age, gender, height, birth, education, etc. These can be distributed to anyone, because everyone will have to fill the same information. Differences usually exist among different objects. One object could have one value for a field, while another may have a different value. Another example of this is a light bulb. The description of a light bulb (its class) has a field indicating that the light bulb is either on or off. However, it is up to the object to decide which one it is. All light bulbs are either on or off, but one light bulb object could be on, while another light bulb object could be off.

What is OOP?

Object-Oriented Programming (abbreviated as OOP) is simply a form of programming centered about the creation of objects and their interactions. OOP can be used to model real-life situations, such as going to the movies or a car factory. Here's the interesting part. In OOP, the creation and interaction of the objects is left entirely up to the programmer. This means that even you can virtually create anything (including cows that jump over the moon and dogs that talk). You can create objects with funny names, states, and behaviors that make no sense at all.

Applications of OOP

Object Oriented Programming is useful because can be used to model situations in real life. Programs written in Object Oriented Languages (OOLs) can also affect objects in real life.

Example: Fan

State

- On/Off (boolean)

- Speed (Intensity, possibly a set of integer)

A fan can either be on or off. Some fans also have speed, indicating how fast the fan is rotating.

Behavior

- Turn on

- Turn off

- Increase Intensity

- Decrease Intensity

You can turn on and turn off a fan. You can also change the speed of a fan if applicable.

Example: Car

State

- Color

- Type (sedan, SUV)

- Model

- Dealer (Kissan, Alkura, Coyota, Pawsda)

- Serial Number

- Number of Seats

- Weight

- Height

A car has different features like color and weight, as indicated above.

Behavior

- Accelerate

- Brake

- Steer

- Turn wipers on

A car can also perform different actions, such as accelerating, braking, steering, and turning the wipers on.

Example: Person

State

- Height

- Weight

- Gender

- Hair color

- Eye Color

Examples of a person's characteristics include their height, weight, gender, race, and eye color.

Behavior

- Eating

- Drinking

- Sitting

- Talking

- Walking

- Running

A person can perform different actions, such as eating, drinking, sitting, talking, walking, and running.

OOP vs. Procedural Programming

Procedural Programming

Procedural programming is merely a type of programming made of step-by-step instructions sent to the computer (called a procedure). The computer carries out those steps. In modern times, procedural programming is not used as much as object-oriented programming.

The following is an example of a procedure that the computer could carry out, or in other words, a procedural program:

OOP

In object-oriented programming, the code of programs is organized in descriptions of objects called classes. Instances of these classes, called objects, are created and interact with each other. Objects have properties and behaviors, much like objects in real life, and represent situations in real life.

Where Java Fits In

Java was designed to be a fast and efficient object-oriented language, or an OOL (recall this from Java's buzzwords in Chapter 1). The code is organized into classes, which are descriptions of objects. This language can represent objects and situations in real life. However, Java also has an element of procedural programming.

For example, the Hello World program in Chapter does not make use of classes or objects. It is just a command given to the computer. Programs that are procedural in nature can also be written in Java. These types of programs are usually limited to the main method of a class since they are only concerned with executing a series of instructions.

OOP in Java

Classes and Objects

Classes are everywhere in Java. Every single program you write is in a class. Classes are meant to make objects, as they are blueprints. However, you do not necessarily have to create an object from the class. This allows the programmer to abstain from the object-oriented aspect of computer programming. An example of this is Hello World. An object is not created from the Hello World program, but it is in a class nevertheless. It is how code is organized in Java.

Classes → Objects

The whole point of Object-Oriented Programming is the creation and interaction of objects. In this section, we will learn how we can create instances of a class (AKA objects). This process is called instantiation. A class simply is a description of an object. Objects can then be created from that description. Here is how one can create an object:

```
CLASS_NAME OBJECT_NAME = new CLASS_NAME
(CONSTRUCTOR_ARGUMENTS);
```

This statement creates an instance (or an object of class CLASS_NAME). Upon the creation of the object, the constructor of the class is called passing any arguments to the constructor.

Fields and Methods

Remember how every object has state and behavior. Well, the state of an object can be described using fields. Fields are like empty buckets placed inside objects. Fields have a name and a value. Look at the following example.

Person Object

Name: John Johnson

Age: 21

Name and age are some of the fields of a person. A class has different fields. Altogether these fields display an object's state. The state of the object above can be described as a twenty-one-year-old male named John Johnson.

```
class Person {

    public void read () {


    }

    public void talk () {


    }

    public void walk () {
```

```
    }

    //... more methods

}
```

Altogether, methods make up the behavior of an object. A person can walk, talk, eat, breathe, and do many more things, as shown above. (Don't worry about the modifiers, such as "public", "void", and the parentheses. You will learn about those in the next chapter.) A Person object should also be able to do these things as well. These actions are represented in the form of methods. An object can do something called "calling a method". That simply means that it does just a certain action. If you perform a method called read, the object will do the action of reading, and go back to executing the rest of the program. Notice that calling a method is an example of an instruction. All instructions go inside methods. Even calling another method must go inside a method. Unlike field declarations, which can exist anywhere, instructions must go inside methods.

There are two special methods: main methods and constructors.

Main Methods

A main method is a special type of method. This method is not required in a class, but it allows you to run the file of that class. A main method is the starting point of a program. It is how the compiler knows where to start executing the program. Let's say you create a class called test and run it. Programs, even object-oriented programs must do something. Main methods are the first one to be called when a class is executed. This method is implicitly called, meaning that you do not have to write in the code that you want the method to be executed; it is automatically called. In addition, main methods have a special name, main. They cannot be renamed; otherwise, the computer will not recognize it as the main method. Here is what a main method looks like within a class.

```
class test {

    public static void main (String [] args) {
```

```
    }

}
```

When you run the class test, then it runs the statements inside the main method. If test has no main method, then the JVM does nothing.

Constructors

A constructor is just a special method of void return type that is called upon the creation of an object from a class. They take care of setting up and "constructing" an object. By default, constructors exist for all objects. However, you can also create different constructors to suit your own needs. Constructors are special for a couple of reasons:

1. They are called automatically upon the creation of a method.

2. Constructors are given the same name as the class they are in.

3. Constructors do not have any return type.

4. The only valid modifiers for constructors are public, private, and protected.

You may need to create a constructor when creating an instance of a Person class to set up a person. You can set the value of different fields essential to the program using the constructor. This is what a constructor looks like in Java.

```
class test_constructor {

    test_constructor () {



    }

}
```

The code above simply indicates a constructor that is called when an instance of test_constructor is created as shown below.

```
test_constructor example = new test_constructor ();
```

The parentheses are included in the instantiation of the class because they are the arguments passed to the method of the constructor. Next, we will show how you can add arguments to a constructor.

You can create multiple constructors in a single class (this is called overloading the constructor). Typically, this is done when you want to provide an option that takes user input to create the object. If you are creating a constructor for the class Car, you may want to allow whoever is creating an object of Car to either pick a color for the car, such as blue or red, or allow him/her to go with any color decided by the class Car. In order to do this, you need to make two methods of the constructor: one that allows the creator to choose the object's color and another that goes with the default values. Just like other methods, constructors also can have arguments. These are passed when the object is created through the parentheses. If class test takes the argument int i, they can be passed as follows.

```
test t = new test (3);
```

However, you cannot create two constructors in a single method that have the same number and type of arguments (in the same order). In addition, if you override a constructor for a class (explicitly declare a constructor), one of the overridden constructors must be used. For example, if you override (create a new implementation of) the default constructor of class test with test (int i), then you may only create an object by passing the arguments of the overridden constructor - int i.

3 Principles of OOP

Object Oriented Programming has three fundamental principles: encapsulation, inheritance, and polymorphism. These principles are put into use commonly in this type of programming. As you continue to learn more about objects, you will likely put these into use frequently.

Inheritance

Think of inheritance like a family tree. Just like a family, classes also have parents and children. Just like a child has characteristics of its parents, a subclass has access to some contents of the parent class.

What is the purpose of inheritance? Well, this proves to be useful when creating a more specific category. For example, you are creating two classes: cats and dogs. These two classes are both examples of mammals, so they will both be warm-blooded and have a backbone. To avoid rewriting the characteristics that these two animals share, it is easier to create a parent class, mammal, and then set dogs and cats as two child classes. As a result, these two classes will both have fields for backbones and spines since their parents have them, but they can also have fields that make them different, such as the food they eat and energy level.

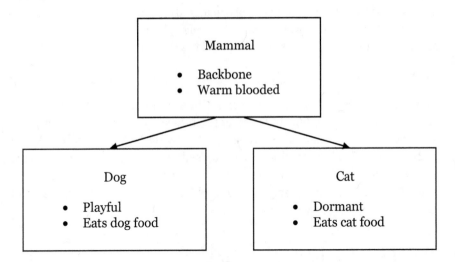

Inheritance in Java

To create a subclass from a class, you need to use a keyword called "extends". This indicates that you are creating a child class. Let's say you are creating a subclass (child) from a superclass (parent), you would type:

```
class Child extends Parent {

CHILD CONTENTS
```

```
HAS ALL THE PUBLIC AND PROTECTED CONTENTS THAT PARENT HAS

}
```

By doing this, class Child inherently gets access to all the public and protected contents of class Parent. Notice that the child class cannot access private fields and members

```
class superclass {

    private String private_String = "This string is private";

    public String public_String = "This string is public";

    protected String protected_String = "This string is
protected";

}

class subclass extends superclass {

    /* This class can access public_String and
protected_String, but not private_String*/

}
```

When you try to run this program, the compiler throws an error because superprivate_String and superprivate_Method are both inaccessible, meaning that they cannot be seen.

Encapsulation

Encapsulation is often referred to as "information hiding". This simply means that objects can access certain objects or parts of objects, but not others.

Access Qualifiers

Access qualifiers are keywords used to modify fields and methods of a class. These are used to control the classes that can access a class's contents.

So, what does access mean? Accessing a field means being able to directly view and change its contents. Accessing a method means being able to call it (execute its statements).

Private

If a field or method is private, then that class and only that class can access that field or method. Let's say that there is a private int, i, within class A. If an instance of A is created in the main method of A, then i can be accessed, such as by being changed to another value. However, if an instance of A is created in the main method of B, then i cannot be accessed. The same thing applies to any other members of A declared private.

Public

If a part of a class is public, that means that any other class inside or outside the package can access it. However, to access a class outside a package, you must access it in the form of package_name.class_name. The name of the other package replaces package_name, and the class you are referring to replaces class_name. An alternative option is to import the package (see Chapter 8). Let's again take the example of a class called A with a public field called i. If an instance of A is created in any class (including A), inside or outside A's package, then i can be accessed and changed to another value.

Protected

If a part of the class is protected, that means that only its subclasses can access it. Let's say class A has a protected int named i. Only A and A's subclasses can access i through an object of A.

Getter and Setter Methods

There are loopholes, though, around access qualifiers. Let's say that you want to allow a method to be able to get the value of a field, but not change it, or change the field of a value, but not know what it is. These things can be done using methods called getter and setter methods.

Getter and setter methods take advantage of the parameters and return types of methods. Getter methods return the value of a variable through the return type, while setter methods take in and set the value of a variable through the parameters.

Why Getter and Setter Methods?

It is useful to use getter and setter methods if variables should not be changed without additional instruction. For example, let's say that you are creating a class that has a method that can multiply two numbers. The class has two fields for those numbers: number1 and number2. Those numbers should only be positive. If those fields are set to be public, another class might come and turn those numbers negative. However, if a setter method is used, then it can stop negative numbers from being set as the value of either number by checking the value taken in through the parameter.

It is also best to use getter and setter methods to avoid abuse of variables. Using these methods is safer than not and makes use of information hiding, one of the major concepts of encapsulation.

Getter Methods

Getter methods allow you to view the value of a field. They do this by returning the value of a variable. For an object to access the value of that variable, it must call the method of that object which then returns that value, as opposed to the object accessing the variable without permission.

Getter methods allow you to view, or "get", the value of a field. For example, if you want an object to be able to access another object's serial number (int serial_number), but not change it, you can provide a getter method. A getter method works by returning the

Let's look at an example.

```
class getter_example {

    int var = 3;

    int get_var () {
```

```
    /*This is a getter method because it returns var.*/

    return var;

  }

}
```

Setter Methods

Setter methods are useful when you want to allow an object to change the value of a field, but also want to maintain some control over that field. To allow a field of an object to be changed through a setter method, that method must take in the new value of that variable through the parameter and set that as the value of that variable.

```
class setter_example {

    int var = 3;

    void set_var (int newvar) {

        /*This is a setter method because it allows you to
change the value of var.*/

        var = newvar;

    }

}
```

Polymorphism

Polymorphism means existing in many different forms. In Java, this comes in the form of overloading, overriding, and as you will see later, anonymous inner classes (Chapter 9). But for now, let's discuss overloading and overriding. These are ways to assign two methods that perform the same function with the same name. Aside from these two cases, two methods or other identifiers rarely have the same name.

Overloading

Overloading means to have different methods with the same name within a single class. This is useful when there are multiple ways to address solving a problem. For example, let's say you want to create a method to add two numbers. The method takes in two numbers as arguments and returns their sum. In Java though, there are several primitive types for numbers. "integer" is a primitive type that can store positive and negative whole numbers. "double" is another primitive type that stores decimal numbers. In different cases, someone will have to either add two whole numbers or two double numbers. As a result, you need two different methods that can add the two different types of numbers. However, these two methods perform the same function: they add two numbers. As a result, you can give them the same name. This is an example of overloading; that is, giving two methods the same name.

However, this concept begs a question: when the method is called, which method does the compiler execute? For the compiler to identify which method is being called, there is a requirement for overloading:

The arguments (AKA Parameters) that a method takes in must differ in number or in type.

Recall that the arguments or parameters of a method are like its input. If this requirement is not met, the compiler will be confused as to which method to execute when the method is called. Think about this for a second. Imagine you are the compiler. You are asked to execute a method. You look at the class of the methods and see that there are two methods that could be executed, both with the same name and both with the same type of arguments. Which one would you pick? After all, both methods can be used to execute the method. The Java compiler would throw an error because it is confused as to which method to execute. Even if the incorrectly overloaded method is not called, the compiler will still identify the methods not fulfilling the requirement for overloading as a possible source of confusion and throw an error.

Here is an example of overloading.

```
class overloading_example {
```

```
//These two are overloaded methods because they have the
same name.

int add (int a ,int b) {

    return a + b;

    //This returns the sum of a and b, an int

}

double add (double a, double b) {

    return a + b;

    //This returns the sum of a and b, a double

}

}
```

Overriding

Overriding is like overloading, except that it deals with subclasses and superclasses. Overriding occurs when a subclass has a method with the same name as a method in the superclass. This technique comes in handy when a subclass has a more specific implementation of that method, whose actions are done for the same purpose.

Let's consider the following example. A species called chewbite eats food by chewing it and biting it. Its subclass, chomp-chewbite eats food by chomping it, then chewing it and biting it. Since the subclass (chomp-chewbite) eats its food differently than the parent class, the method for eating food in the superclass can be overridden by the subclass with the same name. The same task is being done (eating food), but it is done in different ways.

```
class chewbite {

    public void eat () {

        /*Prints "Chew" and "Bite"*/

        System.out.print ("Chew");
```

```
        System.out.print ("Bite");

    }

}

class chompchewbite extends chewbite {

    /*This is an overridden method because it has the same
name as a method of its superclass.*/

    public void eat () {

        /*Prints "Chomp", "Chew", and "Bite"*/

        System.out.print ("Chomp");

        System.out.print ("Chew");

        System.out.print ("Bite");

    }

}
```

Overriding a method is useful when a method accomplishes the same purpose in both subclass and superclass but is done differently.

Super Keyword

In addition, an overridden method of the superclass can also be called from the subclass's method. This is done with the super keyword. This is useful because there is often overlap between the subclass's implementation of a method and the superclass's.

Let's consider the following example. A species called chewbite eats food by chewing it and biting it. Its subclass, chomp-chewbite eats food by chomping it, then chewing it and biting it. Since the subclass (chomp-chewbite) also chews and bites food like its parent class, the superclass's method can be called from the subclass's method.

```
class chewbitev2 {

    public void eat () {
```

```
    /*Prints "Chew" and "Bite"*/

    System.out.print ("Chew");

    System.out.print ("Bite");

  }

}

class chompchewbitev2 extends chewbitev2 {

    /*This is an overridden method because it has the same
name as a method of its superclass.*/

    public void eat () {

      /*Prints "Chomp", "Chew", and "Bite"*/

      System.out.print ("Chomp");

      super.eat();

      /*This calls the implementation of the overridden
method, meaning the eat() method of the superclass. This
command prints "Chew" and "Bite". This saves time in that it
prevents you from having to rewrite the print commands.*/

  }

}
```

Questions

Multiple Choice

1. Which of the following is not one of the principles of object-oriented programming?

    a. Polymorphism

    b. Substitution

    c. Encapsulation

3 Object-oriented Programming

    d. Inheritance

2. Which of the following occurs when more than one method of the same name is added in a class?

    a. Overloading

    b. Overriding

    c. Multiplication

    d. Differentiation

3. Which element of object-oriented programming has to do with many forms?

    a. Polymorphism

    b. Inheritance

    c. Encapsulation

    d. Information-Hiding

4. Which access qualifier allows a field or method to be viewed by classes only within the same package?

    a. public

    b. protected

    c. private

    d. unqualified

5. Which method is automatically called upon the creation of an object?

    a. start ()

    b. constructor

    c. main method

    d. run ()

6. Which method is automatically called when that class is run?

    a. start ()

    b. constructor

    c. main method

    d. run ()

7. What is the superclass of all objects?

```
a. extends
b. java.lang.Object
c. Top_Level_Class
d. java.lang.Class
```

True/False

T F	Superclasses are subclasses, but subclasses are not necessarily superclasses.
T F	Overriding involves creating multiple methods with the same name in a class.
T F	The three principles of object-oriented programming are polymorphism, encapsulation,

	and inheritance.
T F	A subclass does not share any features in common with its superclass.
T F	Subclasses inherit all public, protected, and private contents of their parents.
T F	State describes the characteristics of an object, while behavior describes what it can do.

Free Response

1. What is an object. What are the two elements that all objects have?

2. List the three elements of object-oriented programming.

3. Explain what overloading is and what overriding is. Compare the two. What element of object-oriented programming do these relate to?

4. Explain the concept of inheritance (subclasses and superclasses).

5. What does it mean to access a field or class? List and explain the three access qualifiers, as well as what happens when a field or class is unqualified.

6. Explain what getter and setter methods are, and when they are useful.

7. What is the main method? What is the constructor? How are these two similar? How are they different?

8. Explain what classes are and how they relate to objects.

4 CLASSES AND INTERFACES

In this section, we will go into greater detail about classes, what they are composed of, and what they can do. Interfaces will also be introduced.

Subclasses and Superclasses

Classes are outlines of objects. Sometimes, it happens that these classes also serve as blueprints for other blueprints, for example animals. Animals come in two different categories, mammals, and reptiles. Notice that the classes mammals and reptiles are also subcategories of the class animals, and not only retain the features and behaviors of animals in general, but also have new properties, such as being warm-blooded or cold-blooded.

Since the classes mammals and reptiles are subcategories of the class animals, they would be considered a subclass, and since the class animals is a generalization of the class mammals, it would be considered a superclass. The creation of subclasses from superclasses is called inheritance. Next, we will talk about single and multiple inheritance.

Single inheritance allows the subclass to be derived, or created, from only one class, while multiple inheritance allows the subclass to have more than one parent class (another term for superclass). Java only allows single inheritance to take place. However, a chain of inheritance is allowed. This means that if B is a subclass of A, then B can also have a subclass.

Now let's talk about the features of subclasses and superclasses. Here is a list:

- The subclass has all the features that the superclass does

- The subclass only describes the new features that the superclass doesn't have

- Every subclass is also an instance of the superclass

- Every instance and member of a superclass is also an instance and member of the subclass (constructors are not members)

- Private members of A, the superclass, are not accessible to B, the subclass

How should we go about declaring a subclass? Well, to declare that one class is the subclass of another, we use the keyword extends. For example, if Class A extends Class B, we would type the following, along with any other modifiers that we wish to use.

```
class A extends B {



}
```

Of course, we would have to have another class, B that is already defined. Otherwise, the compiler would give an error.

Fields

There are two parts of classes, fields and methods. As I have mentioned in previous chapters, fields store the state of an object. For example, the state of an aircraft may be its color, size, Vehicle Identification Number (VIN), or location. State can even be a boolean (true or false) value. A boolean state of an aircraft is if it has wheels or not. Remember the keyword *is* or *has* when thinking about state.

Let's now look at an example of an aircraft, a helicopter. Our example helicopter *is* black, *is* 200 square feet, *has* a Vehicle Identification Number of

123456789ABCDEFGH, *is* at coordinates (0.00,0.00), and *has* no wheels (boolean value).

Methods

What are methods?

Methods are used to manipulate the fields of objects and perform other actions. Methods are just a list of instructions for the computer to complete. Some methods have a return type, and others don't. Methods typically have a return type if they are used to give a value back to the user. In addition, some (not all) methods have a parameter, also known as an argument.

Going back to our aircraft class, we can find several different methods that can be created for use by the user. To begin, we can have a method named getLocation. By itself, the name of the method does not return the location, so we have to describe what it does to the program in the method's description. In the scope of the method (in this case, scope means the code within the two curly braces), we can tell the computer to return the value of the location. As was mentioned earlier, the location is a state whose value is stored in a variable. We also need to make sure to specify the return type of the method. Since this method returns an array (a built-in object, which consists of a list of different variables) for the two values, the return type would be an array. Similarly, we can create other methods, getColor, getVIN, and getHasWheels to return the value of Color, VIN, and HasWheels (boolean value).

Return Types

A return type is just an optional variable returned by a method when it is called. The purpose of some methods is to return a value to the caller of the method. For example, let's say there is a method called "Add". The purpose of this method is to find the sum of two numbers and convey this back to the caller of the method. Return types allow this to happen.

For example, if you are creating a method called "Add" (a method that adds two numbers), you will need the method to return to you the addition of those two numbers. What is the purpose of an add function if it doesn't tell you the answer?

```
public int add (int a, int b) {

    return a + b;

}
```

Void

Methods don't necessarily have to return a value to the user. If a method does not return something back to the user, it is labeled with void. The main method in a program is labeled with void because it does not return anything back to the user. You can create a method with a void return type. Examples of methods that have void return types include constructors[3] and main methods.

Use of Return Type

Return types are sometimes used in programs to give back a certain value to the user. This provides useful information back to the programmer. If a programmer needs the value of a certain field that cannot be accessed directly, he/she can call a method that can retrieve the

---

[3] Although constructors are not labeled with the void modifier, they do not have a return value, and one cannot be added.

As shown in the following program, other actions can also be performed on the variable returned. A method call can act as a value of its return type. It can be assigned to another variable or it can call methods of its own.

```
class return_type_example {

    static String get_gibberish() {

        return "randsio ein siaofins e fds";

    }

    public static void main (String [] args) {

        System.out.println(get_gibberish ());

        String random = get_gibberish ();

    }

}
```

Parameters

Some methods have parameters. These parameters are like the input of a function. The parameters of a method are also sometimes known as its arguments. A method can have several parameters. Different parameters can be passed when a method is called different times. Parameters can pretty much take any field. Parameters are usually only taken when there is a need for them. For example, let's say there is a method called add that adds two numbers. This method needs numbers to add. We can tell the computer what two numbers to add via the parameters of the method. That way, the computer can add the two numbers and return the appropriate result.

Parameters are only necessary if the method requires them to perform a certain action to or using that argument. For example, there is a method called double number, whose function is to double the value of a number and return it to the user. The method knows what number to double based on the argument that is provided when the method is called. If a method takes parameters, they go within the parentheses of the method, which are the "(" and ")". If not, there is nothing in between the parentheses: (). This simply tells the computer that the method does not require any parameters. If the method takes in parameters, then the parameters must be passed when the method is called. Otherwise, the compiler throws an error. (There is an exception when methods are overloaded.

By the way, if a method returns some value, it can also perform other actions. Let's look at another example.

```java
public class return_type_example2 {

    static int add (int int1, int int2) {

        /*This method returns the sum of two numbers and prints the string "Add"*/

        System.out.println ("Add");

        return int1 + int2;

    }

    public static void main (String[] args) {

        /*This method calls the add method and prints out the returned int.*/

        System.out.println(add(1,1));

    }

}
```

Here is the output.

```
Add

2
```

Even though the method was called to print the sum of the two numbers, the method also carries out other commands, such as printing "Add" to the console. Thus, keep in mind that even if you only call a method for its return type, other actions may also take place.

Main Methods

Now let's discuss the different forms of methods. Firstly, there are main methods. Main methods have no return type and are called implicitly, meaning that there is no need to call them. When you run a program, the main method of the class you are running is called automatically. When you call a method, you invoke the statements inside them. The only arguments they take in are an array of strings. These arguments are not required for the program to function, unless, of course, the program makes use of these arguments. When you declare a main method, that method is executed automatically when that file is run, hence the name main method. Often times, when you want to write a basic program that doesn't make use of objects, you write the program in the main method.

User Input through the Main Method

You may hear the term "user input" being used throughout this book. That simply means information given by whoever is running the program. Among other ways, this can be done through providing arguments to the main method (if there is one). In Eclipse, this is done by clicking "Run Configurations", and typing in whatever you want in "Program Arguments" under the "Arguments" tab. These arguments are then passed to the main method as an array when it is called. The arguments are divided up into smaller strings called tokens. These tokens are separated by whitespace. Whitespace includes spaces and tabs. Each token is placed in one element of the array. In the body of the main method, the array passed can be manipulated.

```
class main_method_arguments {

    public static void main (String [] args) {

        for (String i: args) {

            System.out.print (i + " ");

        }

        /*This loop iterates through each element of the array

        passed and prints it, inserting a space after each

        element. This should resemble the arguments you
```

```
passed when you ran the main method.*/

    }

}
```

Constructors

Constructors, like main methods, have no return type and are implicitly called. However, constructors are only implicitly called when there is an object being created from the class that holds the constructor. Constructors are special because they have the same name as the class, always (case has to match, too). Constructors may or may not take in parameters, but if they do, you must input the parameters upon the creation of the object. Otherwise, the compiler will give an error. If you do not manually create a constructor, the default constructor is used upon creation of an object. The default constructor sets all the fields to their default value. The default values of variables will be discussed in later chapters.

Superconstructors

A superconstructor is just the constructor of an object's superclass. Every object has a superclass. Even if its class declaration does not use directly tell the computer that you are creating a superclass of another class, all methods are inherently subclasses of a class called java.lang.Object, which is the parent of all classes. Let's say that you want to create a subclass called Cat of class Animal. A cat is just like an animal. Since it is an animal, it would be fair to start off the same way as any other Animal object, and then add any additional features. This would be a good place to call the superconstructor. The superconstructor is just the constructor of the superclass. The superclass can be called via the super keyword. The keyword super indicates that you are referring to the superclass. Here's what calling the superconstructor looks like.

```
super(ARGUMENTS);
```

Of course, it is not required to have arguments, and not all superconstructors do have arguments. You should call the appropriate superconstructor. Here's how you can call a superconstructor that doesn't take arguments

```
super    ();
```

Regular Methods

Lastly, there are regular methods. Some regular methods have return types, and others don't. It depends on what the coder chooses. Similarly, it may or may not take parameters from the user. Unlike constructors and main methods, regular methods are not automatically called. They need to be explicitly called by the programmer.

Abstract Classes

An abstract class is a class that contains one or more abstract methods. An abstract method is a method that has no implementation (i.e. there is no body of the method). If an abstract method is in a class, then the class becomes an abstract class. Both the class and the method must be preceded with the label "abstract". This tells the computer that the abstract method is intentionally left without a body. An abstract class cannot be instantiated (i.e. you cannot create an object from an abstract class), except through an anonymous class (Chapter 9). Here is what an abstract class looks like.

```
abstract class abstract_demo {

    abstract void to_be_implemented ();

    void another_nonabstract_method () {

        INSTRUCTIONS

    }

}
```

Interfaces

C++ provides a feature called multiple inheritance, which is a way of deriving one class from many. Unlike classes, they are not programs on their own, but instead only contain methods (no constructors/main methods) with no implementation. The implementation of a method is just its body (i.e. the statements within the two curly braces) As a result, interfaces themselves cannot be compiled and executed, unlike classes.

In addition, they are either public or unqualified (recall these from access qualifiers). Unqualified means that there is no access qualifier preceding it. Keeping an interface's methods private or protected does not make sense, as these would prevent interfaces from being used by other classes, the sole purpose of an interface. Although inheritance like in subclasses and superclasses is allowed, instances of interfaces cannot be declared, and their fields are all static (once per interface) and final (they cannot be changed). You do not have to explicitly modify the methods of interfaces as static or final.

So, what good are interfaces? Well, other classes depend on interfaces for commonly used methods. Those classes must declare public versions of the methods in the interface. They are declared like classes, except with the keyword "interface". Classes can put interfaces to use via the "implements" keyword. They can implement many interfaces as long as their names are separated by a comma followed by a space. Here is an example of an interface and a class that uses that interface.

```
interface wheels {

    void front_left_wheel (boolean forward, int speed);

    void front_right_wheel (boolean forward, int speed);

    void back_left_wheel (boolean forward, int speed);

    void back_right_wheel (boolean forward, int speed);

}
```

These methods are provided a body in the class that implements them.

```
class car implements wheels {

    public void front_left_wheel (boolean forward, int speed)
    {

        //code to move forward or backward at a certain speed
```

```
    }

    public void front_right_wheel (boolean forward, int
speed) {

        //code to move forward or backward at a certain speed

    }

    public void back_left_wheel (boolean forward, int speed) {

        //code to move forward or backward at a certain speed

    }

    public void back_right_wheel (boolean forward, int speed) {

        //code to move forward or backward at a certain speed

    }

}
```

Interfaces are useful when there are many classes with many of the same methods. Those methods can be generalized to a single interface, where many classes can use the same methods.

A class can both extend a superclass and implement interfaces. A class can implement more than one interface.

There are interfaces provided in libraries, which will be discussed later on.

Questions

Multiple Choice

1. Which of the following is used by a method to take in input?

    a. overloading

    b. arguments

    c.   return type

    d.   return statement

2. Which of the following is used by a method to return input to the user?

    a.   overloading

    b.   arguments

    c.   return type

    d.   return statement

3. Which keyword is used to modify a field to make it immutable?

    a.   static

    b.   void

    c.   final

    d.   same

4. Which of the following are interfaces allowed to do?

    a.   Declare their methods final

    b.   Declare their methods static

    c.   Be declared public

    d.   Be instantiated

5. Which keyword is used to create a subclass of another class?

    a.   implements

    b.   void

    c.   static

     d. extends

True/False

T	F	Superclasses are subclasses, but subclasses are not necessarily superclasses.
T	F	Overriding involves creating multiple methods with the same name in a class.
T	F	Methods in interfaces have no implementation
T	F	It is possible to run the main method of an interface.
T	F	An abstract class is the same thing as an interface.
T	F	The main method takes no parameters
T	F	Abstract classes cannot be instantiated

Free Response

1. Compare abstract classes and interfaces.

2. What's wrong with the following code?

```
interface steer {

    public void turnRight ();

    public void turnLeft ();

}

class car extends steer {

    public void turnRight () {

        CODE TO TURN RIGHT

    }

    public void turnLeft () {

        CODE TO TURN LEFT

    }

}
```

5 THREADS

What is a Thread?

A thread is simply a sequence of instructions given to the computer. Threads are created whenever you run a program. When you run a program in Java, you are just calling the main method of a class. Thus, a thread is created for the main method of that class.

However, it is also possible for the programmer to create threads manually. In Java, the java.lang library has everything you need in order to create a thread. Just like many other features of Java, threads are also created via classes. When you create threads in Java, you are actually creating instances of a class. You can then call methods of those classes to get the threads going. Java allows you to create multiple threads at a time.

Multithreading

Multithreading is exactly what it sounds like. It is a feature that combines multiple threads into a single program. Using this feature is most useful when a program needs to accomplish two logically separate tasks at once.

Java allows multithreading to take place. The programmer just has to create and run multiple threads at once. The CPU then goes from thread to thread doing its job.

Analogy: Two Doors

The CPU is like one person. Imagine a room with two doors that face opposite ways. The CPU has to print "Open" when either one of them opens. The CPU can only look at one door at a time and check to see if it is open, since it cannot see in two directions at once. Multithreading does not give the CPU two pairs of eyes that can look at both doors at once. Instead, it allows the CPU to alternate between doors really fast. That way, the computer can spin around really, really fast, allowing it to see one door, and then the other almost immediately. As a result, the computer knows right away when a door is opened.

Example

For example, imagine a program that creates a frame with two buttons. When you press the first button, it prints "Button 1". When you press the second button, it prints "Button 2". You, the programmer, need to make sure that the program is constantly keeping an eye on both those buttons such that in the event that either one is pressed, it can respond and print the appropriate statement. For this, the program can use threads. That way, the CPU, can alternate between checking both buttons as opposed to just one.

Multithreading vs. Multiprocessing

Multiprocessing has to do with running separate tasks using two or more processors. Recall that a processor is the "brain" of the computer that is responsible for executing most of the tasks. Creation of many processes is often a time and resource consuming task.

On the other hand, threads are much faster. Many threads can be run on the CPU, unlike multiprocessing, which involves more than one processor. Threads are all executed within a single process, and unlike the creation of processes, which consumes much time and resources, the creation of threads is much quicker. Threads are lightweight, meaning that they can share resources with other threads.

How to Create Threads

As I mentioned before, Java allows the programmer to create threads. This can be done in a couple different ways. One involves implementing methods of an interface called Runnable. The other involves creating a subclass of a class in java.lang called Thread. This class also implements the interface Runnable.

Implementing java.lang.Runnable

If you choose to implement the Runnable interface, you will have to implement a method called run(). This method has no return type. It is called either directly by the user or by another method called start(). The start() method is usually called by the user when he/she wants the thread to start the thread. Unlike the run() method, this method can only be called once. You do not need to override the start method. Here is an example of a thread that implements java.lang.Runnable

```
public class threads implements Runnable{

    public void run() {


    }

}
```

Extending java.lang.Thread

The Thread class in the package java.lang also implements the Runnable interface described above. The Thread class is different from just any class that implements Runnable because it has additional features in the form of methods and constructors.

The Thread class has eight different constructors that take in different parameters, such as a string for the name of the thread and an object implementing Runnable. All the constructors will not be covered in detail in this book. There is, however, a simple constructor that takes in no arguments. This simply creates a new Thread object.

This class also has methods that turn out to be useful when coding.

Some of these are static. These methods are used to provide information about all the threads that are being run in a program. For example, currentThread () returns the Thread that is currently running in a program. sleep (long millis) is another static method that allows you to pause the execution of the current thread for a specified number of milliseconds (taken in as the parameter). yield () is another static method that tells the scheduler that the current thread can give up execution. The scheduler, however, does not have to follow this.

There are also other methods created for individual thread objects (they are non-static). start () is a method called by a thread that simply gets the thread started. This method can only be called once per thread, and this method calls the run () method. The run () method consists of that object's thread of instructions. This method can be called more than once, unlike the start () method. It is overridden and consists of that object's thread of instructions. Of course there are other methods of this class, but they won't be covered in this book. If you wish to find more information about this class and its methods, you can visit the website (http://docs.oracle.com/javase/8/docs/api/) containing descriptions of all the libraries, their fields, and their methods.

The import statement

The import statement is simply a commmand that allows you to refer to elements of a package, such as java.lang.Thread or java.lang.Runnable using a shorter name. Instead of using the long versions of the name, you can simply refer to them as Thread or Runnable. The syntax of this statement is import followed by a package name. In this case the package is java.lang. To import all the elements of java.lang, simply write import java.util.* before the class declaration.

```
import java.util.*;

class threads extends Thread {
```

```
}
```

Threads in Java

Sharing Resources

What if two threads want to share resources. Let's say there is a text file titled File1. This file is empty. There is a separate class titled Manipulation that holds two threads in its main method. Both threads try writing messages to each other. Number 1 writes a message. Number 2 reads Number 1's message and writes another message. Number 1 again reads Number 2's message and writes another message. This process goes on. However, there is an issue. How does Number 1 know when Number 2 is finished reading and writing, and how does Number 2 know when Number 1 is finished. This is an issue that comes up when two objects share resources, such as threads.

Fortunately, there is a simple solution to that. Threads can use locks on their objects to prevent the other thread(s) from taking it before they are done.

Synchronized Keyword

The synchronized keyword is a keyword used in Java to prevent two threads from accessing one resource at the same time. This comes in two forms: a synchronized block, and a synchronized modifier.

Synchronized Block

A synchronized block of code is simply a block of code inside a method that takes a parameter. This block of code then places a lock on that object (taken in as a parameter) until the statements within the body of the method are executed. Here's what this looks like:

```
synchronized (object_name) {

    //The statements here must be executed before

    //object_name can be accessed again
```

}

Synchronized Modifier

This modifier is used before methods to indicate that only one thread can access it at a time. If a thread is currently using the method, then another thread must wait until the other is done running the method. This is used before the return type of a method.

```
public synchronized void my_method () {

    //SYNCHRONIZED STATEMENTS

}
```

Lock Object

Notify, Notify All, Wait

notify (), notifyAll (), and wait () are all methods of class Object used while working with threads. These also all relate to the resource sharing of threads.

void wait ()

This method causes the current thread to wait until another thread calls the notify () or notifyAll () method for that object. In that case, the current thread then waits until it can again get ownership of that object.

void notifyAll ()

This method tells all threads waiting on an object to wake up. This warns the thread that the object is about to be relinquished and that the thread should be ready to take possession of it.

void notify ()

This method is similar to the notifyAll () method. However, it is different in that it only wakes up a single thread. This is chosen randomly by the computer. The thread then waits until the object is unlocked and is available to be unlocked. This has no effect on the thread's ability to obtain a lock on the object (if there are more threads waiting to lock the object).

Deadlock

Deadlock occurs when two threads are both waiting for a resource that the other has. This sometimes occurs when working with threads, especially with more complicated programs.

Priorities

Every thread is assigned a priority when it is created. A priority simply indicates how urgently a thread needs to be executed. Threads with higher priorities are executed first. However, there is a limit to how much and how little priority can be given to a thread.

MAX_PRIORITY

MAX_PRIORITY is a static, final integer of the class java.lang.Thread that indicates the greatest priority a thread can have (in the form of a number). This number is 10.

MIN_PRIORITY

Just like the MAX_PRIORITY, the MIN_PRIORITY shows how little priority can be given to a thread. This number is 1.

NORM_PRIORITY

NORM_PRIORITY is a number that indicates the default priority given to a thread. This is the original priority of a thread when it is created. This number is 5.

Daemon Threads

Allow the JVM to exit even while the threads are still running void setDaemon (boolean on)

boolean isDaemon ()

Daemon threads are special types of threads that can continue running even after Java exits runtime.

Uses

Daemon threads are useful in some cases, such as garbage collection.

There are a couple of methods belonging to class Thread that you can use to decide whether a thread is a daemon or not.

void setDaemon (boolean on)

If the argument passed when this method is called is true, then the thread is a daemon, and the JVM can exit while this thread continues to run. If the argument passed is false, then this thread is a non-daemon thread, and keeps the JVM running as long as it is running.

boolean isDaemon ()

This method returns a true or false value depending on whether a thread is a daemon or not. If it is a daemon, then it returns true. If not, then it returns false.

Example

Here is an example of how the CPU splits its time between two threads.

```
class thread_1 extends java.lang.Thread{

    public void run () {

        for (;;) {

            System.out.println ("t1");
```

5 Threads

```
        }

    /*This method prints t1 in an infinite loop so that we
know exactly when the CPU is executing this thread*/

    }

}

class thread_2 extends java.lang.Thread{

    public void run () {

        for (;;) {

            System.out.println ("t2");

        }

    /*This method prints t2 in an infinite loop so that we
know exactly when the CPU is executing this thread*/

    }

}

class thread_test extends java.lang.Thread{

    public static void main (String[] args) {

        thread_1 t1 = new thread_1 ();

        //This creates a new instance of the thread_1 class
shown above

        thread_2 t2 = new thread_2 ();

        //This creates a new instance of the thread_2 class
shown above

        t1.start ();

        //This command starts the execution of t1.

        t2.start ();

        //This command starts the execution of t2.
```

}

}

If you run thread_test, you should notice that the CPU's work never ends; it constantly has to print t1 and t2. Because there is only one console, the CPU takes turns printing from t1, and then moves to t2.

Questions

Multiple Choice

1. What is a thread in computer programming?

    a. A special type of method in a program

    b. A subset of String

    c. A primitive type

    d. A way to run the main method

2. How many threads does the main method for the Hello_World program create?

    a. 1

    b. 2

    c. 3

    d. 4

3. What library is the Thread object from?

    a. java.lang

    b. java.util

    c. java.io

    d. java.awt

4. What is the name of the thread that allows the JVM to exit even while the thread is running?

    a. monster

    b. daemon

    c. synchronized

    d. holdup

5. Which is NOT a way to create a thread in Java?

    a. Run the main method of a class

    b. Extend the Thread class

    c. Create a method that throws an exception

    d. Implement the Runnable interface

True/False

T F	A thread is automatically created when you run the main method of a program in Java.
T F	There is no limit to the minimum and maximum priority a thread can have in Java.
T F	Daemon threads cannot keep

		running once the JVM stops.
T	F	There is no system for sharing resources, such as a file, in Java.
T	F	Deadlock is an impossible situation in Java.
T	F	The Thread class in Java is abstract.
T	F	Java allows programmers to multithread.

Free Response

1. Create two thread classes. One should be called thread_one and the other should be called thread_two. When thread_one is started, it should print "thread one" forever. When thread_two is started, it should print "thread two" forever. Make observations. What do you see? How often does the computer switch between threads?

2. Experiment with priorities. Using the program from above, assign thread_one to a higher priority than thread_two. Make observations.

6 EXCEPTIONS

What are Exceptions?

In Java, things don't always go as planned, and we have to be ready to handle the problems that arise in those cases. For example, we may be asked by the user to open a file that does not exist. We have no idea what the user will ask us to do at compile time. As a result, we do not know if there is going to be an error until runtime. This is an example of an exception. An exception (short for exceptional condition) is a problem that occurs when the program is run and prevents the program from executing normally.

Exceptions vs. Compilation Errors

Recall that compilation is just the conversion of Java code into bytecode. Here, the computer can detect errors in syntax or semantics of the program, such as to put a semicolon at the end of a statement or using a variable that was never declared/assigned. These are all errors that are easy to detect because the compiler gives these errors only when it has trouble understanding your code.

Exceptions, however, are different from compilation errors because they occur at runtime. Usually, they include areas that the compiler does not check thoroughly. For example, you can declare an array and then reference an index that goes out of its bounds, such as:

Object[] a = new Object[1];

a[4] = new Object();

You can write this code (in the main method of course) and compile it without error. This does not make sense because you cannot set the value of an object that does not exist in the array. But the compiler does not see anything wrong with the code, so it does not throw an error. When it comes time to execution of the code, though, the JVM sees that the program is trying to assign the value of an object that does not exist. After all, the array only contains one Object, so it is impossible to assign the fifth object of the array. An exception is thrown (specifically an ArrayIndexOutOfBoundsException exception) because there is a runtime error.

Exceptions in Java

The Exception Class

Just like many other things in Java, Exception is also a class in Java. It has a superclass called Throwable. Throwable is the superclass of errors and exceptions in Java.

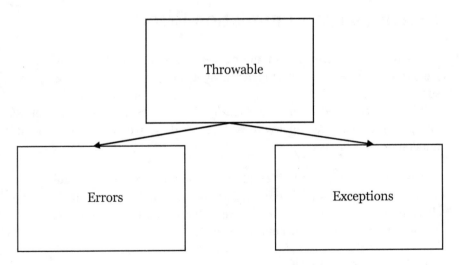

Exceptions are "thrown" either automatically when an exceptional condition occurs or manually. Here are examples of situations where exceptions are thrown.

- Reference to nonexistent files

- Running out of memory

- Loss of a network connections

When these events occur, an exception is thrown. An exception is simply an object that can cause a program to stop running, unless handled appropriately by a "try/catch" statement.

The "Throwable" class is a hierarchy. Not all exceptions are direct subclasses of "Throwable", but are objects of classes somewhere down the inheritance line. "Throwable" has two important subclasses: errors and exceptions. The difference between the two is that exceptions can be handled at runtime, but errors cannot. Errors also indicate more serious problems. For example, if you forget to include a semicolon after one of your statements, it is an error.

We are dealing with exceptions so we will disregard errors for now. Exceptions also have two categories, checked and unchecked. Checked exceptions are monitored by the compiler, while unchecked compilers are not monitored. An exception is not only automatically produced by the compiler, but can also be manually thrown, as we will see shortly

Subclasses of Exception

There are also subclasses of the class Exception in Java designed for more specific purposes. There are several of these subclasses in Java that cover a broad range of topics. Some of these subclasses have other subclasses that cover even narrower topics. For example, the ArrayIndexOutOfBounds Exception is an exception that occurs when the programmer refers to an element of an array that goes out of that array's index. This is a subclass of IndexOutOfBounds Exception, which is applicable in more general situations, such as when a String or Vector, or any index refers to an element beyond its index. Many of these are associated with the AWT and IO packages.

Programmer-Generated Exceptions

The programmer can also generate exceptions in a program. This can be done if the programmer feels that an exception should be thrown if some event occurs, but there is no run-time problem identified by the JVM

For example, a programmer may want to manually generate an exception if .

Throw and Throws Keywords

Exceptions are manually thrown via the "throw" and "throws" keyword.

This keyword is used in two places: the scope of the method and the declaration of the method. Throw is a command that goes inside the scope of a method. This is followed by an exception object, and tells the computer to "throw" that exception object. Throwing an exception is also a command, so the throw keyword must go inside a method. After the throw statement, the method stops execution, unless, of course, it is surrounded by a try/catch statement, in which case, it goes to the catch block.

If a method throws an exception, then the method must have the throws keyword. One exception to that is if the throw command in the method is surrounded by a try/catch statement. In that case, the throws keyword does not have to be used in the method declaration. However, the throws keyword can be used even if the method does not throw an exception. This keyword comes right before the scope of the method. But if a method that uses the throws keyword is called by another method, one of two things must happen: either the method calling the other method must throw the exception, or a try/catch statement must be used. Here is what a method that throws an exception looks like:

```
public void throwing throws Exception {

    throw new Exception ();

}
```

Handling Exceptions: Try/Catch Statements

Now, let's get to the part where we handle the exception. Try/Catch statements are ways that you can prevent the program from stopping if an exception is thrown. The format is simple, it looks like the following:

```
try {

    CODE SUSPECTED OF THROWING AN EXCEPTION

}

catch (exception_class exception_name) {

    WHAT TO DO IF AN EXCEPTION IS THROWN

}
```

As you can see, if the programmer thinks that some code might throw an exception, it is placed within a try block. If it does indeed throw an exception, it goes to the catch block. The catch block takes an exception object as its argument. If the class of the exception that is thrown matches the class within the catch block, then the computer begins to execute the statements instead of the try block, rather than stopping the program. You can think of exceptions like an airplane crash. Using try/catch blocks allows a gentle, padded landing, as opposed to an abrupt and rough stop (not using try/catch).

Many catch blocks can be used for a single "try" block, if there are no statements in between. In addition, any name can be used for the exception object name in the parameter of the catch block, just like in a method.

finally block

The finally block is simply a block of code after a try/catch statement that is to be executed regardless of whether an exception is thrown or not. If an exception is thrown, then the finally clause is executed after the catch statement. If not, it is executed after the try statement. The point of a finally block is to allow the programmer to execute some code that must be executed in both cases.

One alternative to the finally block is placing the code that must be executed in both situations both in the catch block and after the try/catch statement because the code will be executed if an exception is thrown and even if not. However, this causes repetition of code, which is not recommended.

Here is what the finally block looks like.

```
try {

    CODE SUSPECTED OF THROWING AN EXCEPTION

}

catch (exception_class exception_name) {

    WHAT TO DO IF AN EXCEPTION IS THROWN

}

finally {

    EXECUTED REGARDLESS OF WHETHER AN EXCEPTION IS THROWN

}
```

Handling Exceptions: Foolproofing Code

Even though you do not know when most exceptions are about to take place, you can make your program less prone to exceptions by foolproofing it. Foolproofing code simply means making it sturdier to avoid exceptions. You cannot make a program foolproof to all exceptions, but you can make it foolproof it to some.

You can use try/catch statements to keep the flow of the program, it is usually used as a last resort, meaning that you should only use it when you absolutely must.

Example: Handling ArrayIndexOutOfBounds Exceptions

Let's foolproof some code to avoid the ArrayIndexOutOfBounds Exception. All arrays are objects, so they have a field called length. You can use this field to make sure that you don't reference an element out of the array's bounds, even if you don't assign the length of the array yourself.

A good example of this would be the arguments passed by the user through the main method (recall this from Chapter 3). This is represented as an array consisting of strings. If the arguments passed by the user consist of three words separated by spaces, then the array String [] args will also have three different elements. For example, this is args (user input) becomes ["this", "is", "args"] (String [] args).

You may be writing a program that recreates the user's arguments passed in the main method. You know that the user's input consists of an array of Strings. The original user input would be a string of those three strings separated by spaces. To do so, you can write a loop that strings together the arguments.

```
class exception_unhandled {

    public static void main (String [] args) {

        String s = "";

        for (int i = 0;;i ++) {

            /*No condition, the loop never stops until an
exception is thrown*/

            s += args[i];

            s += " ";

        }

    }

}
```

As you can see, the loop above the loop above never stops; there is no condition. "i" just continues to increase and increase. At some point, it is inevitable that i will be greater than the index of args []. No array can be infinitely long. Then, s will be trying to add to itself an element of an array that does not exist. Let's say args has an index of 4. When i reaches 4, then the program is in trouble (args [4] does not exist, there is no fifth element). An ArrayIndexOutOfBoundsException will be thrown. Let's handle this exception two different ways.

Try/Catch

We can insert a try/catch statement into the loop so that when the exception is thrown, it can be handled appropriately.

```
class exception_caught {

    public static void main (String [] args) {

        String s = "";

        for (int i = 0;;i ++) {

            try {

                /*No condition, the loop never stops until an
exception is thrown*/

                s += args[i];

                s += " ";

            }

            catch (ArrayIndexOutOfBoundsException e) {

                break;

                /*Once the exception is thrown, the loop is
broken, and the rest of the code continues execution*/

            }

        }

    }

}
```

When the compiler throws an exception, then the program handles this appropriately and breaks out of the loop. You can even print the string when it is finished. try/catch statements like these can be used to keep the program going.

Foolproofing

As I said earlier, using try/catch statements is a last resort. You should not use them unless you have to. In this case, there is a better way to write the

6 Exceptions

same program. We can add a condition to the for loop so that the statements only loop as long there is a next element present in the array. This can be done using the length field of all arrays.

```
class exception_foolproofed {

    public static void main (String [] args) {

        String s = "";

        for (int i = 0;i<args.length;i ++) {

            /*The loop will stop execution after i has reached
the last element of the index*/

            s += args[i];

            s += " ";

        }

    }

}
```

As you can see above, i stops just before it equals the length of the array. (Remember that the indexing of arrays starts at 0, so the maximum index is length-1.) It continues to add elements of the array to the big string, followed by a space. This is the most effective way to go about recreating user arguments.

Questions

Multiple Choice

1. What is the most direct superclass of the class Exception?

    a. Executable

    b. Object

    c. Runnable

    d. Throwable

2. When are exceptions thrown?

    a. compile-time

    b. when the program is written

    c. runtime

    d. when a program is written

3. How can an exception be appropriately handled if it arises during the execution of a program outside the control of the programmer?

    a. return statement

    b. try/catch statement

    c. the debugger

    d. careful proofreading

4. What keyword is used to indicate that a method may generate an exception?

    a. return;

    b. throws;

    c. throw;

    d. break;

5. Match a problem that could arise in a Java program to either an error or an exception.

    a. A non-existent element of an array is referenced; error

    b. A semicolon is not added to the end of a statement; exception

c. A method is called with the wrong parameters; exception

d. A method is called on an object initialized to null

True/False

T F	A programmer cannot generate and throw his/her own exception.
T F	Only one exception can be handled per try block.
T F	Foolproofing code can help make it less prone to exceptions.
T F	The throw keyword is used in the declaration of a method to indicate that the method may generate an exception, while the throws keyword generates an exception.
T F	Most exceptions can be detected at compile-time, unlike errors, which occur only at runtime.

Free Response

1. Compare errors and exceptions.

2. Create a method called throwing that throws an exception called MyException (you will have to create the class for this first). From the

main method of that class, create an instance of the class and call throwing on that method. Appropriately handle the exception with a try/catch statement. When the exception is caught, print "caught" to the console.

3. Explain what the ArrayIndexOutOfBoundsException is and when it is thrown.

7 NESTED CLASSES

What are nested classes?

A nested class is a class within another class. They are one exception to the rule that only one class goes in a file. Nested classes prove to be useful in a variety of circumstances. There are several types of nested classes in Java, and they all have different restrictions and uses.

Here is what a nested class looks like in Java.

```
class outer_class {

    class nested_class {

        // THIS IS A NESTED CLASS

    }

}
```

Why nested classes?

Organization

Sometimes, it happens that some classes are only useful because they are used with or fulfill some purpose of another class. Placing a class within a related class allows for more organized code, including better code organization and readability.

Testing Purposes

Certain nested classes can be used to test features of a class. Testing for a program is usually accomplished through a separate program that checks that program's features. Using nested classes to test a program not only keeps all code in one place, making it easy to control, but also makes it easier for the programmer to make changes to the program, if required.

Categories of Nested Classes

There are two main categories of nested classes: static and non-static (inner) classes. These two branches serve very different purposes, as you will see soon.

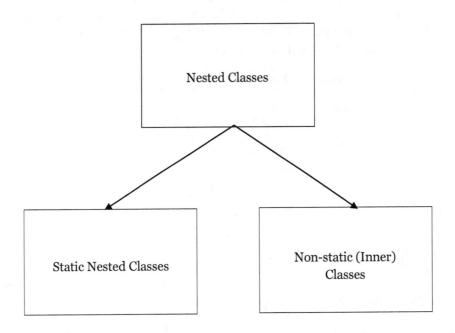

Static Nested Classes

7 Nested Classes

In the context of classes, a static class is an independent part of the class (not a field) that can contain the same components as any other class, such as extending other classes, implementing interfaces, containing fields, methods, etc. A static class is a class inside another class with the static modifier behind it. Here's what it looks like:

```
class outer_class {

    OUTER CLASS CODE

    static class static_nested {

        STATIC CLASS CODE

    }

}
```

As you can see, it is just a class within a class with static modifier behind it. They can have a main method, so it can be run as an independent class. These two classes are independent of each other, so each can be instantiated just like any other object.

To compile and execute a static nested class, you need to use the "$" symbol. Just like the "." symbol is used to reference elements of a class, the "$" symbol is used to run a static class of another class. Here is how it is used.

```
OUTER_CLASS$STATIC_ CLASS
```

This is used to tell the computer that STATIC_CLASS is not its own class within a package, but is within another class. You cannot use STATIC_CLASS to compile and execute STATIC_CLASS like it is any other class. You have to use the format OUTER_CLASS$STATIC_CLASS.

To run a static class in Eclipse, select "Run Configurations" and type in the class name (OUTER_CLASS$STATIC_CLASS) to run the program.

When instantiating a static class, though, a programmer can use "." to reference the static class.

```
OUTER_CLASS.STATIC_CLASS STATIC_OBJECT_NAME = new
OUTER_CLASS.STATIC_CLASS ();
```

Since a static class is within another class, it can be used to test the outer class's features by creating an object of that class, and can be deleted just as quickly when the program is done being tested.

Non-Static Nested Classes

The second category of nested classes is non-static nested classes, sometimes called inner classes. These classes can be inside methods, unlike static methods. Like fields of a class, non-static nested classes can also be givne similar modifiers. Inner classes are members of the class or object in which they are enclosed. These can be divided into two categories: regular inner classes and anonymous inner classes.

Inner Classes

Inner classes are like non-static fields of the enclosing class. They are simply descriptions of objects that can be instantiated given that there is an object of the outer class. After all, non-static members only exist when there is an instance of the outer class. Like fields, they can be given modifiers, such as public, private, protected, and final. Here is what an inner class looks like.

```
class outer {

    class inner {

        INNER CONTENTS

    }

    public static void main (String [] args) {

        outer o = new outer ();

        inner i = o.new inner ();

        //This is how you instantiate an inner class.

    }

}
```

An inner object is declared in the following format. An instance of the outer class is needed to instantiate the inner class.

```
INNER_CLASS INNER_CLASS_NAME = OUTER_OBJECT.new INNER_CLASS
();
```

Since this field is not an object, but a class, it essentially has no functionality until an object of the outer class is created, just like you need an object to call a class. From there, an instance of the inner class can be created. For this reason, the scope of the class may also contain constructors to control what happens when the object is created.

However, this class may not be run as an independent program. The reason is simple. An inner class is like a non-static field of a class. It only exists as a member of an existing object of the outer class. Since the existence of an outer object requires a program to be currently running, there is no possible way to run this inner class in a new program, since this will not exist without an instance of the enclosing class. Nonetheless, a method called main may still be declared, it just won't be implicitly called.

Anonymous Inner Classes

Anonymous inner classes are a way of creating an instance of a class with contents modified from the original class.

For example, you can create an instance of Car, but make the methods do different actions without changing the class description. The class Car will stay the same, but the object behaves differently. It will still be an instance of the class Car, but it will have different capabilities. Let's take an example.

An imaginary car dealer is willing to give you a car that can paint itself any color other than red. (see class below)

```
class car2 {

    String color;

    /*The following is a method that paints a car any color
but red*/
```

```
public void paint (String color) {

    if (color != "red") {

        this.color = color;

    }

}

}
```

But what if you want 9 cars that can't paint themselves red, but 1 car that can paint itself red. You can't change the original car class, because then all 10 cars will be able to paint themselves red. To solve this problem, you can create an instance of an anonymous class for Car. Only that instance will be different, while all other instances will stay the same as before.

Here is the syntax for an anonymous class in Java. (Notice the semicolon at the end of the assignment.)

```
Class_Name Object_Name = new Class_Name () {

    CLASS DESCRIPTION

};
```

Creating anonymous classes is sort of like taking a shortcut to creating an independent subclass and overriding the required methods. The class created has the properties of the original class and retains those described in the anonymous class's description. For example, it can override methods of the original class. When that object's method is called, then the overridden method will be called.

Anonymous classes are different in that they have a separate class description, but the class itself does not have a name, hence making them anonymous. They simply override methods of a certain class under the name of that class. All

You can think of an anonymous class like a subclass of another class. It can modify the contents of its superclass, such as through overriding methods. However, there are limitations to anonymous classes. These classes are only useful for overriding methods of the superclass and setting new values to the fields. New methods and fields can be created, but are not useful. The computer will not recognize these, as they are not present in the original class. As a result, you cannot write

```
Object obj = new Object () {

    /*Object does not have a method titled new_method*/

    void new_method () {

        System.out.println ("Something new");

    }

};


obj.new_method ();

/*THIS CODE WILL NOT COMPILE*/
```

However, you can write something very similar to achieve the same thing.

```
new Object () {

    /*Object does not have a method titled new_method*/

    void new_method () {

        System.out.println ("Something new");

    }

}.new_method ();

/*THIS CODE WILL COMPILE (IN THE MAIN METHOD OF A CLASS)*/
```

In general, it is best to use anonymous classes only to override existing methods, since the compiler only recognizes fields and methods of the original class most of the time.

Going back to the painting car problem, you can create an anonymous class of Car that can paint itself red like this. This overrides the method of the original class, allowing the car to even be painted "red".

```
class car2_anony {

    car2 special_car = new car2 () {

        public void paint (String color) {

            this.color = color;

        }

    };

    /*This car is special because unlike other instances of
car, this one can paint itself red*/

}
```

Anonymous classes may not contain constructors or main methods. The reasons are fairly self-explanatory.

By creating an anonymous class, you are essentially overriding the contents of the original class and instantiating it. That modified class is similar in that it contains all the same fields and methods, but is also different as the methods of the class may have different implementations. This produces a very similar effect as creating a subclass of the original class and then instantiating it. However, if you pay attention, you will notice that this modified class is not given a separate name. Even though it has different contents than the original class, its class is the original class. Since this "subclass" has no name, a constructor cannot be created for that class. In addition, the compiler does not recognize the original class's name as the constructor, as the anonymous class is not the original class; it is a subclass.

The main method is never implicitly called, either. The anonymous class is not a member of the enclosing class, either; the object is. As a result, the anonymous class cannot be run as a program. In addition, the only purpose of the anonymous class is for overriding the methods and changing the fields of the original class. The class is only useful for that object.

Super Keyword

Since an anonymous class acts like a subclass of an original class, the super keyword can also be used in anonymous classes to refer back to the original class that is modified. Let's take a look at an example. Here we'll override the toString () method of Object and call the overridden method using the super keyword.

```
class anony_super {

    public static void main (String[] args) {

        Object obj = new Object () {

            public String toString () {

                String s = super.toString() + " overridden!";

                return s;

            }

        };

        System.out.println(obj.toString());

    }

}
```

Here is a sample output from this program.

```
anony_super$1@76ccd017 overridden!
```

As shown in the program above, the overridden toString () method calls the toString () method of the Object class, adds " overridden!", and returns the string.

Instantiating Abstract Classes using Anonymous Classes

Abstract classes are classes are simply classes that contain one or more method declared abstract (it has no implementation). Abstract classes are only useful because it can have children that are a little more useful and override the abstract methods. As was discussed earlier, anonymous classes sometimes serve as subclasses of the original class. So, abstract classes can now be instantiated, given that the abstract methods are given an implementation when it is instantiated. Here is an example.

```
abstract class abstract_class {

    abstract void method1 ();

    abstract void method2 ();

}

class anony {

    public static void main (String[] args) {

        abstract_class ac = new abstract_class () {

            void method1() {

                //Implementation for method1

            }

            void method2() {

                //Implementation for method2

            }

        };

        /*Abstract classes can be initialized with anonymous
classes, as long as the abstract methods are given an
implementation.*/

    }

}
```

Questions

Multiple Choice

7 Nested Classes

1. What is another term for a non-static nested class?

    a.   anonymous class

    b.   inner class

    c.   nested class

    d.   static class

2. Which of the following is not an example of a nested class?

    a.   static class

    b.   member class

    c.   inner class

    d.   anonymous class

3. What symbol is used to reference a static nested class?

    a.   .

    b. $

    c.   x

    d.   *

4. What keyword is used in an anonymous inner class to refer back to the original class?

    a.   orig

    b.   super

    c.   implements

    d.   extends

5. Which of the following nested classes can have a main method that is automatically executed?

a. inner class

b. static class

c. anonymous class

d. member class

True/False

T F	The super keyword can be used in anonymous inner classes to refer to the original class.
T F	You can execute a static class, but not an inner class.
T F	A static class can create an instance of itself and the outer object.
T F	You need an object of the outer class to instantiate the inner class.
T F	The dollar sign can be used to create an instance of a static nested class.

Free Response

1. Compare and contrast static nested classes and inner classes.

2. List and explain some benefits of nested classes.

3. Create an anonymous inner object of java.lang.Object and override the String toString () method to make it return "new String". Call this method on this new object and print the result.

4. Why are anonymous inner classes called anonymous?

8 LIBRARIES

Libraries are a collection of commonly used routines. Java has many, many libraries. There are so many that they cannot all be covered in this section. Therefore, only the most common and important libraries will be discussed. The following are built-in libraries. For this reason, they are preceded by java and a period.

```
import package1.package2.class_name;
```

This imports a class from package2, which is a package within package1.

Third-party libraries built by people not involved with Java also exist. You can find these libraries online.

What are Libraries?

Simply put, libraries are collections of classes and interfaces created for a specific purpose. Libraries are organized into packages and provide the programmer with resources that he can use while programming. Libraries are created because they are widely used. Programmers can use these libraries to do certain tasks without having to rewrite code. For example, programmers often have to use a random number. A method in the java.util library has a random number generator so that programmers do not have to write the code for a random number every time they need a random number. They just have to call the method for a random generator.

Java's libraries are divided into packages and subpackages. Packages contain classes, interfaces, and sometimes even more specific packages. Those "more specific packages" are called subpackages. Subpackages are just like packages, except they are within other packages.

Java standard libraries (also called core libraries) are the libraries created along with the Java language. These are built into the Java language and are downloaded with the JDK.

A description of these methods for all the libraries are in the Javadoc for each class. You can also find the actual code of each library using your IDE. In addition, docs.oracle.com contains a package summary for each and every package that exists.

This section will cover the important classes and concepts of some of Java's built-in libraries. However, this will not be a comprehensive list, as Java has way too many libraries to be discussed. You will learn the applications of some of Java's most frequently used classes.

Deprecated Methods

Java is an ever-changing language. As time goes on, Oracle continues to make changes to the libraries and their code and methods. Sometimes, Oracle decides that they are going to deprecate an old method that perhaps was not as effective or that they are replacing with a new method. If a method is deprecated, it is regarded as out of date. These methods can still be used by the programmer, but it is best to not use them. After all, the owners of Java probably had some reason to deprecate the method. Usually, the deprecated method is substituted with something better. There is a special tag (@deprecated) added to deprecated methods in their Javadoc (recall that this is a special comment tool). This book does not cover deprecated methods (as of Java 8).

Importing Packages

Some of Java's libraries are built in, meaning that they are downloaded along with the JVM. Your computer already has access to all these classes, interfaces, and their methods. Now you, the programmer, can put these libraries to use.

Importing a package simply allows you to refer to a class using a shorter name, as opposed to a longer name. By importing a library at the beginning of a file, you are just telling the computer that in the rest of the class, you may refer to the class with an abbreviated name. Java classes are organized in packages. You can import several packages at a time in a single class.

The Import Statement

The import statement allows you to either import all the classes in a package (using the "*" symbol) or a certain class in a package. For example, let's use a random number program. Let's say you are writing a program that prints out a random number. To get a random number, you have to use the class java.util.Random, which has a method that generates a random number. Here is the code for that kind of program.

```
class random_number1 {

    public static void main (String[] args) {

        System.out.println (new
java.util.Random().nextDouble());

    }

}
```

Writing the full package name (java.util.Random) is a bit tedious, isn't it (especially if you have to rewrite it several times)? Well, importing the class (java.util.Random) or all the classes in java.util (java.util.*) makes it much easier to refer to the class.

OPTION 1: IMPORTING ALL CLASSES IN PACKAGE JAVA.UTIL

```
import java.util.*;


class random_number2 {

    public static void main (String[] args) {

        System.out.println (new Random().nextDouble());
```

```
    }

}
```

OPTION 2: IMPORTING ONLY THE RANDOM CLASS IN PACKAGE JAVA.UTIL

```
import java.util.Random;


class random_number3 {

    public static void main (String[] args) {

        System.out.println (new Random().nextDouble());

    }

}
```

As you can see, importing one or many classes allows you to refer to just the class name (Random), as opposed to the full name (java.util.Random). As you continue to learn and get more experienced with the Java language, you will find that the import statement is actually quite helpful in programs.

In Java, you import a package before the declaration of a class, as I have shown above. I previously mentioned that all Java code goes within a class declaration. However, the import statement is one exception.

java.util

The "util" part of this library comes from "utilities" of Java. These include the collections framework (methods and algorithms for arrays and other objects), a random number generator, date and time facilities, and event models (responds to events such as mouse clicks and typed keys).

Queue

8 Libraries

A queue is a type of list usually with a First In First Out (FIFO) Format. You can think of a queue as a line. You get in the line first, you get out of the line first. Similarly, you add objects to a queue, and the first one to go in and what goes out. You can control what goes in and out using methods, which will be discussed shortly.

In Java, there is an abstract class for a Queue, called AbstractQueue, and an interface called Queue. Remember that an abstract class is a class with one or more abstract methods (methods labeled abstract and left without implementation). You cannot create an instance of an abstract class in Java.

To create an instance of a queue, there are a few things you can do.

1. Create a separate class called Queue (or whatever you want to tell you that it is a class for queue) and make it a subclass of AbstractQueue. Then, you can add all the unimplemented methods of AbstractQueue, such as boolean offer (Object e), Object poll (), Object peek (), and int size ().

2. You can also create a class that implements java.util.Queue. Be careful what you name your class. If you name your class Queue, make sure to clarify to the computer that you want to implement java.util.Queue, not the Queue class you are declaring (class Queue implements java.util.Queue)

AbstractQueue Methods

Built In

boolean add (Object e)

The add method does what it sounds like. It attempts to add an Object that it takes in its parameters (e) into the queue. If this is successful, the method returns true. If not, the method throws an exception (IllegalStateException e).

void clear ()

This method is also self-explanatory. It simply clears any elements in the queue.

Object element ()

This method returns the first Object added to the Queue. The first element added to the queue is also known as the head of the queue. If there is no Object to get from the queue, it returns an exception. (NoSuchElementException e).

Casting Objects in a Queue

You can also add something called a cast to methods. For example, if you add 5 instances of "Car" to a queue, and use element () to get them back, the computer only knows that you are getting 5 objects, not 5 cars. This is because the return type of element () is Object. If you are sure that the object you are getting back is in fact a Car (subclass of Object), then you can use a cast and call one of the methods of Car or assign its value to another instance of Car.

```
class Queue_Example {

    public static void main (String[] args) {

        Queue q = new Queue ();

        /*Let's say there is another class called Queue that is
a subclass of AbstractQueue and implements all its abstract
methods*/

        car car1 = new car ();

        q.offer(car1);

        car car2 = (car) q.element();

        /*element () returns an Object instance, not a Car
instance, so a cast must be added because we are sure that
this element is an instance of Car.*/

    }

}
```

Object remove()

This method removes and returns to the user the head of the queue. If there is no method to remove, it throws an exception (NoSuchElementException e).

Left Abstract

boolean offer (Object e)

This method is very similar to add (Object e) - see above. There is only one difference. It returns true if e is successfully added to the queue (like add (Object e), and returns false if otherwise (unlike add (Object e)). This method does not throw any exceptions.

Object poll ()

This method removes and returns to the user the head of the Queue. If there is no Object to return, it returns null, meaning that the object is empty. (compare to remove())

Object peek ()

This method is the same as element (), except that it does not throw an exception. It returns the head of the queue. If there is no head to return, the method returns null.

int size ()

This method returns the size of the queue.

java.util.Queue

The Queue interface is simply an interface containing the implementationfor the abstract methods mentioned above, as well as a few others. Those additional methods will not be covered in this book.

Stack

A stack is like a queue. It is a list, but it has a Last In First Out (LIFO) Format. You can think of a stack in computer science like a stack of papers. You put the paper down in the stack first and put several other papers down on top of it. The paper that you put first in the stack (the one on the bottom) will be the last to come out. Imagine that you can then only remove one paper at a time.

boolean empty ()

This method returns true if the stack is empty. If the stack is not empty, then it returns false.

E push (E item)

This method adds an item to the top of the stack. E is simply a "type parameter in Stack". For the purpose of this book, E is the same thing as an object. This method returns the parameter (E item).

E pop ()

This method returns and then removes the item at the top of the stack (i.e. the item last pushed onto the stack using push (E item)). Notice that the head of a stack is different than the head of a queue. The head of a stack is the tail of a queue, and the tail of a stack is the head of a queue. These two are different because they have different. Queues are FIFO, while Stacks are LIFO.

E peek ()

This method returns without removing the item at the head of the stack.

int search (Object o)

This method simply returns the location of an object in the argument (Object o) from the top of the stack. The head of the stack is 1, the second-in-line is 2, and so on. If o is not an object in the stack, then -1 is returned.

Here is an example of a stack put to use.

```
import java.util.Stack;


class Stack_Example {

    public static void main (String [] args) {

        Stack s = new Stack ();


        s.add(new Object () {

                public String toString () {

                    return "Object 1";

                }

        });


        s.add(new Object () {

            public String toString () {

                return "Object 2";

            }

        });


        s.add(new Object () {

            public String toString () {

                return "Object 3";
```

```
        }

    });
```

```
    /*Anonymous class put to use. toString () method
overridden for each method. This is done to help identify the
obejcts.*/
```

```
    Object o = s.pop();
```

```
    /*o is the Object popped from the top of the stack.
Since the object with the toString () method that returns
"Object 3" was added last, it will also be popped first.*/
```

```
    System.out.println(o.toString());
```

```
    /*This prints "Object 3" since this is what the
"toString ()" method of the popped object returns.*/
```

```
    }

}
```

Random Number Generator

java.util.Random is a class that has methods that generate random numbers. To do this, first create an instance of this class. Then, you can call methods of that class to generate random values.

int nextInt (int bound)

This method returns a random integer from 0 to the specified integer, bound.

int nextInt ()

This method returns a random integer.

double nextDouble ()

This method returns a random double.

float nextFloat ()

This method returns a random float.

long nextLong ()

This method returns a random long.

boolean nextBoolean ()

This method returns a random boolean value.

Date

The Date class is a class in java.util that is used for keeping track of time. This class has fields for the year, month, day, hour, minute, second, and millisecond. This class does not track the progression of time, meaning that the value of the Date object does not change with time. Once you set the value of Date that is what it remains unless you change it. However, new objects can be created using information on time obtained from other sources. The fields indicating the time are non-static, meaning that different times can exist for different Date objects. In addition, you can set the date of a Date object to any value you want, even if the date to which you are assigning the object is not the same as the current time.

One way you can set the time in the Date class is using the number of milliseconds that have elapsed since January 1, 1970 at 00:00:00 GMT. The class then takes care of converting the total number of milliseconds to find the exact date and time you are referring to. For this, you will have to find the time that has elapsed since 1970 and calculate the milliseconds yourself, and the Date object will turn that number back into the date (year, month, day, hour, minute, second, millisecond).

Constructors

The Date class currently has two non-deprecated constructors. Those include Date () and Date (long date).

Date ()

This constructor just creates a new Date object and sets it to the current time. This date does not change with the time.

Date (long date)

There is also a constructor with which you can set the current date. long date is a primitive type, with which you can set the date. date represents the number of milliseconds that have elapsed since January 1, 1970 at 00:00:00 GMT. You can tell the computer this number, and it knows the exact date and time by converting the number of milliseconds to year, month, day, etc.

Methods

boolean after (Date when)

This method tests whether the current date is after the when Date in the parameter or not. If the current date occurs after Date when, then the method returns true. If not, the method returns false.

For example, let's say the current time is January 1, 2000. The when Date is December 31, 1999. Even though the current time is just slightly ahead of the Date in the parameter, it returns true.

boolean before (Date when)

This method is the opposite of after (Date when). Instead of testing whether the current date is after the when Date, it tests if the current date occurs before the when Date. This returns true if the current date occurs before when, and false otherwise.

int compareTo (Date anotherDate)

This method is like the after (Date when) and before (Date when) methods combined. This method compares the date calling the method to another date (Date anotherDate) taken in as the parameter. If the two dates are equal, then 0 is returned. If the date calling the method is before anotherDate, then a value less than 0 is returned. If the date calling the method occurs after anotherDate, then a value greater than 0 is returned.

boolean equals (Object obj)

This method overrides the equals method of class Object. If the Date object calling the method has a year, month, day, hour, minute, second, and millisecond equal to the object in the parameter, then true is returned. Else, false is returned.

long getTime ()

This method simply returns the number of seconds that have elapsed since January 1, 1970 at 00:00:00 GMT for the date returning the method.

void setTime (long time)

This method is the counterpart of getTime(). Instead of getting the time for a particular date, you can set the Date (taken in as a parameter). You can call this method more than once and set different values for Date.

toString()

As you probably know by now, almost all classes in the Java libraries override class Object's toString() method. Date is interesting because instead of converting it to something like Date@11aa1111, it tells you the date in the form of "DAY_OF_WEEK MONTH DAY_OF_MONTH HOUR:MINUTE:SECOND TIME_ZONE YEAR". You can test this feature out yourself with different Date objects.

Here is an example of the Date object.

```
import java.util.Date;
```

```
import java.util.Date;


class Date_Example {

    public static void main (String[] args) {

        Date d = new Date ();


        d.setTime(1483257600000L);

        //The date is set to the number of milliseconds since
1970


        System.out.println(d.toString());

        //Overridden toString () method of the Date class
provides the date

    }

}
```

HashMap

HashMap is a useful tool used for linking two values and allows fast lookup. Let's say there are students at a school. Each of those students has their own ID. As a result, the ID can be used to identify a worker. This is an example of where a HashMap should be used. Again, a HashMap is used to connect two values. One value is called Key and the other value is called Value.

Key	Value
83804	John Doe

83805	Rick Smith
83806	Billy Bob Joe

A key can be used to find a certain value.

V put (K key, V value)

This method simply maps a key to a value. If key already exists, then value is set as the new value for the key, and the old value is returned to the user. If there was no value previously mapped to the key, then null is returned. K and V are simply Objects. That's all you need to know for now.

void clear ()

This method simply clears any keys and maps in the HashMap

boolean containsKey (Object key)

This method returns true if the HashMap contains a key specified in the argument. Else, it returns false.

boolean containsValue (Object value)

This method returns true if the HashMap contains a value specified in the argument. Else, it returns false.

V get (Object key)

This method returns the value that maps to the key specified in the argument. If there is no key matching the argument, or it maps to a null value, it returns null.

boolean isEmpty ()

This method returns true if there are no keys that map to any values in the HashMap. Otherwise, it returns false.

V remove (Object key)

This method removes key from the HashMap, if it is present. It returns the value associated with key.

boolean remove (Object key, Object value)

This method removes key from the HashMap, if it is present and currently mapped to value. True is returned if key is removed. If not, false is returned.

V replace (K key, V value)

This method replaces the value of key with value, specified in the parameter, as long as key is currently mapped to some value. It returns the previous value that mapped to key.

boolean replace (K key, V oldValue, V newValue)

This method sets newValue as the new value of key if oldValue is the current value that maps to key. If successful, then true is returned. If not, then false is returned.

int size ()

This method returns the number of keys mapped to values there are in the HashMap. A key mapped to a value counts as one.

Here is an example of a HashMap.

```
import java.util.HashMap;
```

```
class HashMap_Example {

    public static void main (String [] args) {

        HashMap h = new HashMap ();

        //Creates a new HashMap


        h.put("John Doe", "83804");

        h.put("Rick Smith", "83805");

        h.put("Billy Bob Joe", "83806");

        //Places three keys and their values into the HashMap


        System.out.println(h.get("John Doe"));

        //Prints the value for the key "John Doe"

    }

}
```

Scanner

A scanner simply reads input from a source. A good example of this is System.in. To provide input to System.in, simply type text into the Console box.

For example, notice that you can also type text into the Console of your IDE. This is a source of input called System.in. You can write a program that uses a Scanner to scan the text you have written in the Console box. However, scanners are not just limited to system input. Scanners can also read input from a file, a path, an InputStream object, or Readable object. Different constructors take in different arguments. Constructors of this class include: Scanner, (File source), Scanner(InputStream source), Scanner(Path source), Scanner(Readable source), and Scanner(String source). All these arguments are examples of what a Scanner can read (there are others that exist).

Closing the Scanner

void close ()

This is a method of void return type that simply closes the scanner. By closing the scanner, you are no longer able to perform search operations using the scanner. When you perform search operations on the Scanner, they do not take place immediately; they take place after a buffer of time. The computer decides when they take place. This is done for efficiency reasons. By closing the scanner, you tell the computer to immediately perform those actions.

Delimiters

A Scanner divides strings into tokens. Tokens are the different parts that make up a sentence. In the sentence "I love cats," The tokens are "I", "love", and "cats" because they make up the sentence. But how do we know where tokens start and where they finish? In English, words are separated by spaces. That's how we differentiate between them. Similarly, the Scanner differentiates between tokens using delimiters. A delimiter is just a pattern that separates different words. In English, a space in a delimiter. In Java, the default delimiter is a whitespace. Whitespace is just space in between words that does not have any characters. This includes spaces, tabs, and new lines. Any space that does not have text is whitespace. So, Scanners separate words using whitespaces.

I   love

cats.

The sentence above is separated by whitespaces (a tab and a new line). This consists of the tokens "I", "love", and "cats". This is the Java Scanner's default delimiter. However, you, the programmer, can also change the delimiter. Look at the following sentence

Izlovezcats.

There are no whitespaces in the preceding string, so a scanner would take this as a single token, Izlovezcats. However, the three tokens ("I", "love", "cats") are separated by the letter z. In Java, you can change the delimiter to whatever you want (including the letter z). If z is the delimiter in the string above, then the tokens would be "I", "love", and "cats".

Pattern delimiter ()

This method returns the delimiter that is currently being used. By default, this is a whitespace. This returns an object of class Pattern. Pattern is simply another class of java.util. To find out the string being used as the delimiter, call the String pattern () method of the Pattern object. This returns to you the delimiter currently being used.

Scanner useDelimiter (String pattern)

Using this method, you can set the pattern being used as a delimiter. This simply takes in an argument for the pattern, and sets it as the delimiter. There is an overloaded form of the method that takes a Pattern object, and sets its pattern as the delimiter – ScanneruseDelimiter (Pattern pattern). This method returns the Scannerobject that calls the method.

Searching

String findInLine (String pattern)

This method attempts to find a certain pattern in the input and returns the text that matches the pattern. An overloaded form of this method exists that takes a Pattern object as its argument - String findInLine (Pattern pattern). If the Scanner is closed and this method is called, then an IllegalStateException is thrown.

Next Token

The following methods are used to get information about the next token if it exists. These methods all throw an IllegalStateException if they are called while the Scanner is closed.

boolean hasNext ()

This method returns true if there is another token left to scan in the input. If not, the method returns false.

String next ()

This method returns the next token in the input. A NoSuchElementException is thrown if there is no token left to scan.

hasNext (String pattern)

This method returns true if the next token matches the String in the argument and returns false otherwise.

Next Line

These methods throw an IllegalStateException if they are called while the Scanneris closed.

boolean hasNextLine ()

This method returns true if there is a next line of input left to scan. If not, false is returned.

String nextLine ()

This method returns the rest of the line, and then skips to the next line (if there is one). If there is no next line, then it throws a NoSuchElementException.

This method waits until there is a line of text in the console before reading the String. It is not executed if your cursor is in the same line as that text.

Finding a primitive type

The Scannercan also identify if the next token can be interpreted as a certain primitive type, including boolean, byte, double, float, int, long, and short.

8 Libraries

These methods all throw an IllegalStateException if they are called while the Scanner is closed.

boolean hasNextBoolean (), hasNextByte (), hasNextDouble (), hasNextFloat (), hasNextInt(), hasNextLong (), hasNextShort ()

These methods return true if the next token, if there is one, can be interpreted as a primitive type (depending on the method). If not, it returns false.

boolean nextBoolean (), byte nextByte (), double nextDouble (), float nextFloat (), int nextInt (), long nextLong (), short nextShort ()

These methods scan the next token and attempt to convert them to the respective primitive type and return them. If they cannot be interpreted as the indicated primitive type (calling nextBoolean () when the next token is "2"), then it throws an InputMismatchException. If there are no tokens left to scan, then a NoSuchElementException is thrown.

Here is an example of a program using Scanner.

```
import java.util.Scanner;


class Scanner_Example {

    public static void main (String [] args) {

        Scanner s = new Scanner (System.in);

        /*This creates a new Scanner with input coming from
System.in. To give input to this source, simply type text into
the Console box and move to the next line.*/


        System.out.println(s.nextLine());
```

175

```
    /*Once you type text into the console, the Scanner will
read this, and print the same string*/

    }

}
```

java.io

"IO" stands for "Input Output". This library links Java programs to the rest of the computer. This is done in several ways, including files and data streams.

This section introduces data streams, and reading and writing to data streams, specifically focusing on files.

Files

A file is an example of a data source to which you can read and write. Here is some information about classes that you can use while programming. A file is just a piece of data stored on your computer. Like objects, they also have identifiers, and other information. For example, saving a document on Notepad is an example of creating a file. The Java programs that you write on your computer are also files. In Java, File is an object, just like many other things.

Directory

Every file has something called a directory. A directory simply indicates the location of a file. Just like there are hierarchies of inheritance in Java, there are different levels of organization in a computer's memory. Files are usually stored on the hard disk of a computer. Within that, there are usually several folders that organize that computer's information. Common ones include "Documents" and "Downloads". In order to work with files on a computer, it is necessary for you to be familiar with the organization of your computer, as this differs from system to system.

boolean canExecute ()

This method returns true if the file can be executed by the Java Virtual Machine.

boolean canRead ()

This method returns true if the file's contents are able to be read. If not, it returns false.

boolean setReadable (boolean readable)

This method attempts to change if a file can be readable. If this is successful, the method returns true. If not, it returns false.

boolean canWrite ()

This method returns true if the contents of the file exist and can be modified. Otherwise, the method returns false.

boolean createNewFile ()

This method attempts to create the file specified by the pathname, if it does not exist. A program cannot create a file that already exists. If successful, the method returns true. Otherwise, it returns false.

boolean mkdir ()

This method makes a directory specified by the pathname. If the directory is created, true is returned. Otherwise, false is returned.

boolean delete ()

This method deletes the file or directory specified by the pathname. This method returns true if the operation is successful, and false otherwise.

void deleteOnExit ()

This method deletes the file just as the JVM exits.

String getAbsolutePath ()

This method returns a string that represents the full pathname of a file. An example of an absolute path is "C:\Users\Doe\Documents\Test.txt". The backslashes represent the subdirectories leading up to the file. Remember that a file is in a directory and there can be multiple directories within each other.

String getName ()

This method returns the name of the file, excluding the directories and subdirectories. An example of a file name is "Test.txt".

boolean isDirectory ()

This method returns true if the pathname of a file represents a directory. Otherwise, false is returned.

boolean isFile ()

This method returns true if the pathname represents a file. Otherwise, false is returned.

Here is an example of the File object

```
import java.io.File;


class File_Example {

    public static void main (String [] args) {

        File f = new File
("C:\\Users\\RandomGuy123\\Documents\\NewDocument123");
```

```
        /*This creates a new File object with the specified
pathname. This is different for each computer, so make sure
that yours is correct for your computer.

        In addition, recall that a backslash has a special
purpose in Java. If your pathname has a backslash, make sure
to make that two backslashes, as shown in the example, so the
computer understands that the backslash is part of the
string.*/



        f.mkdirs ();

        /*Makes the file, along with any required parent
directories. This will return false if your pathname already
leads to an existing file.*/

    }

}
```

Data Streams

What are Data Streams?

A data stream is just information that flows to or from a source, much like how rivers flow in a lake. That information is connected to a data source. An example of a data source is a network or file. They are called sources because they are the origin ("source") of information.

You can read and write to data sources. Reading means taking in information from a data soure and converting it into primitive types.

FileReader

Files are composed of character streams. A character stream is just a type of data stream composed of characters as opposed to other data. A data stream of a file, such as a text document, is just a flow of characters in a document. Using data streams, we can read those files.

Constructors

FileReader (String fileName)

This constructor creates a new reader for the file whose name is specified in the argument.

FileReader (File file)

This constructor creates a new reader for the file specified in the argument.

boolean ready ()

This method returns true and only true if the stream can be read. Else, it returns false.

int read ()

This method returns an integer representing the next character read in the input stream. You can cast that int into a char like so

char c = (char) 115;

This char represents 's'.

void close ()

This method simply closes the stream. After this is called, you can no longer read or write to the stream.

```
import java.io.*;

//Many classes of java.io are used, so all are imported for
simplicity


class File_Reader_Example {

    public static void main (String [] args) {
```

8 Libraries

```
        File f = new File
("C:\\Users\\RandomGuy123\\Documents\\NewDocument123");

        /*File object for the FileReader to read*/



        FileReader fr = null;

        /*Declaration and assignment of a FileReader. You'll
see soon why this is set to null*/



        try {

            fr = new FileReader (f);

        /*Assigning FileReader to its value, a FileReader that
takes a File object as its argument. There is a chance that
statements within this try block are not executed. The
computer knows that it is possible that an exception may be
thrown before fr is assigned a value. As a result, assigning
it a temporary value outside the try block lets the computer
know that it definitely has a value, thus allowing you to call
methods on the object, and perform other actions*/

        } catch (FileNotFoundException e) {

            e.printStackTrace();

        }

        /*Preparing in case an exception arises*/



        try {

            for (;;) {

                int i = fr.read();

        /*An integer representing the next character

        is stored in an int, i*/

                if (i != -1) {
```

```
            System.out.print ((char) i);
/*If i != -1, meaning that the end of file is
not reached, then a character is printed*/

        }
        else {
            break;
/*If i == -1, meaning that the end of file is
reached, then the loop stops*/

        }

    }
} catch (IOException e) {
    e.printStackTrace();

}
/*Preparing in case an exception arises*/


try {
    fr.close();
/*Closing the stream so that it is flushed and
so the resources can be freed*/
} catch (IOException e) {
    e.printStackTrace();

}


/*Try this program out with a text document*/
```

```
    }

}
```

FileWriter

Constructors

FileWriter (String fileName)

This constructor creates a new writer for the file whose name is specified in the argument.

FileWriter (File file)

This constructor creates a new writer for the file specified in the argument.

void write (int c)

This method writes a single character to the stream. c is an integer that represents a character.

void close ()

Like the method in FileReader, this method simply closes the data stream, flushing it first and freeing all its resources.

Here is an example of a FileWriter object.

```
import java.io.*;

class File_Writer_Example {

    public static void main (String[] args) {

        File f = new File
("C:\\Users\\RandomGuy123\\Documents\\NewDocument123");

        /*File for the FileWriter to write to write to*/
```

```
        FileWriter fw = null;

        /*Declaration and assignment of FileWriter. FileWriter
is declared and assigned outside the try block for the same
reason that FileReader was. Read on to find out why*/


        try {

            fw = new FileWriter (f);

            /*Assigning FileWriter to its value, a FileWriter
that takes a File object as its argument. There is a chance
that statements within this try block are not executed. The
computer knows that it is possible that an exception may be
thrown before fw is assigned a value. As a result, assigning
it a temporary value outside the try block lets the computer
know that it definitely has a value, thus allowing you to call
methods on the object, and perform other actions*/

        } catch (IOException e) {

            e.printStackTrace();

        }


        try {

            fw.write("Hello File Writer");

            /*Writing a string to the file via a data stream*/

        } catch (IOException e) {

            e.printStackTrace();

        }


        try {

            fw.close();
```

```
        /*Closing the stream so that the string is flushed
through the stream and so that the resources can be freed*/

    } catch (IOException e) {

        e.printStackTrace();

    }

  }

}
```

java.lang

"java.lang" is the library responsible for the tools important for the Java language. Some classes from this library include "Class", "Object", and "Math".

String

Recall from Chapter 3 that a string is just an object. Just like any other class, the String class has methods.

Wrapper Classes

What are wrapper classes?

Wrapper classes are used to enclose a primitive type into an object. They are simply object representations of primitive types, such as byte, short, int, long, double, float, and boolean. Each wrapper object has a field for that primitive type.

Examples of wrapper classes in Java include Byte (to wrap around primitive type byte), Short (to wrap around short), Integer (to wrap around int), Long (to wrap around long), Double (to wrap around double), Float (to wrap around float), and Boolean (to wrap around boolean). Pay attention to the case of these classes compared to the primitive type.

These wrapper classes also all have a method called valueOf (primitive_type identifer). This method, of course, varies depending on the primitive type it wraps around. For example, the class integer has the static method valueOf (char c), while Integer has the method valueOf (int i). This method returns a wrapper object for that particular class with the value passed in the argument of that method. For example, when Character.valueOf ('c'); is called, then a Character object with value 'c' is passed.

In addition, the value of these wrapper classes can be set equal to the primitive type. For example, one could write Double d = 0.0; or Integer i = 0;.

Why wrapper classes?

Wrapper classes are used because they are objects and allow primitive types to be used in different ways. For example, wrapper classes allow primitive type values to be added to a Collection, such as lists, queues, and vectors (which only take objects) or an array of objects. In addition, wrapper classes provide some useful methods. For example, the Double class has a static method called compare (double d1, double d2) that allow the programmer to compare two doubles to find the larger.

Boolean

Boolean is the wrapper class for the primitive type boolean. To set the value of this wrapper class to a boolean value, you can use the constructor Boolean (String s). This boolean value of this object is only true if the string taken in as the parameter of the constructor is equal to "true". If not, the value is set to false, regardless of the value of the string. The case does not matter when passing the string (i.e. you can pass "True" and not "true", and still have the object be set to true).

In order to get the value of this primitive type, use the method booleanValue () on the Boolean object.

Byte

Byte is the wrapper class of the primitive type byte. In order to set the value of this object, simply use the constructor Byte (byte value). This sets the value of the wrapper class equal to the value passed in as the argument of the constructor.

To get the primitive type value of this object, call the byteValue () method of the class. This simply returns the primitive type value held by the object. You can also get double, integer, float, long, int, and short primitive type values through the methods byteValue (), doubleValue (), floatValue (), intValue (), shortValue (), and longValue ().

Character

Character is the wrapper class of the primitive type char. Like the other two wrapper classes, you can set the primitive type value through the constructor: Character (char value). You can get the primitive type value of this object by calling charValue ().

Double

Double is the wrapper class for the primitive type double. The value is set through the constructor: Double (double value), and can be retrieved through doubleValue ().

Float

Float is the wrapper class for the primitive type float. This method has two constructors through which you can set the value. One is Float (float value) and the other is Float (double value). Both these primitive types can be used to set the value of this object. In addition, you can get both the double and float values through doubleValue () and floatValue ().

Integer

Integer is the wrapper class for the primitive type int. You can only set the value for this object using an int argument - Integer (int value), but you can retrieve byte, double, float, int, short, and long values of the object through byteValue (), doubleValue (), floatValue (), intValue (), shortValue (), and longValue ().

Long

Long is the wrapper class for the primitive type long. The constructor for this wrapper class is Long (long value). Like the Integer class, you can call byteValue (), doubleValue (), floatValue (), intValue (), shortValue (), and longValue ().

Short

Short is the wrapper class for the primitive type short. The constructor for this class takes a value to which the object is set - Short (short value). This can also return byte, double, float, int, short, and long values - byteValue (), doubleValue (), floatValue (), intValue (), shortValue (), and longValue ().

Math

The Math class allows you to easily perform several mathematical operations you may need to in a program. A few methods from this class will be covered. A few methods that cover advanced topics will be omitted, since you will probably not be expected to know them.

int abs (int a)

This method returns the absolute value of an integer. Absolute value means making the sign of a number positive. The absolute value of -5 is 5 and the absolute value of 5 is 5. Alternate forms of this method exist that return the absolute value of a number: double abs (double a), float abs (float a), and long abs (long a).

int addExact (int x, int y)

addExact (int x, int y) is a method that returns the exact addition of two integers. Another form of this method that adds and returns two long primitive types is long addExact (long x, long y).

double cbrt (double a)

This method returns the cube root of a double. If you haven't learned what a cube root is, do not worry.

int decrementExact (int a)

This is a method that returns an integer after subtracting one from it (decrementing). An overloaded form of this method that decrements a long primitive type is long decrementExact (long b)

int incrementExact (int a)

This is a method that returns an integer after adding one to it (incrementing). An alternate form of this method that increments a long primitive type is long incrementExact (long b)

int min (int a, int b)

This method returns the smaller of the two integer values. Alternate forms of this method include long min (long a), float min (float a), and double min (double a).

int max (int a, int b)

This method returns the larger of the two integer values. Alternate forms of this method include long max (long a, long b), float max (float a, float b), and bould max (double a, double b).

int multiplyExact (int x, int y)

This method returns the exact multiplication of two integer values. This can also be done with long primitive types - multiply Exact (long x, long y)

int negateExact (int a)

This method negates a number. A negative number becomes positive, and a positive number becomes negative. The same can be done with long primitive types - negateExact (long a)

double pow (double a, double b)

This method returns a double whose value is a raised to the power of b. If you have not learned about exponents, do not worry.

double random ()

This method returns a random number greater than or equal to 0.0, and less than 1.0.

double rint (double a)

This method rounds the argument to the nearest integer and returns it as a double.

int round (double a)

This method rounds and returns the argument to the nearest integer. The same can be done for float primitive type: round (float a)

double sqrt (double a)

This method takes the square root of a double argument and returns it. If you have not learned about square roots, do not worry about this.

int subtractExact (int x, int y)

This method simply subtracts y from x and returns the value. Another form of this method that returns the difference of two long primitive types is subtractExact.

Object

Object is a class. That is a bit confusing, but the creators created a class called Object to represent all Objects in the Java programming languages. After all, everything is an object. Every single class in Java is a subclass of the class Object (except the class Object). Even though you may not use the extends keyword, all classes in Java are subclasses of the Object class. Even if you extend another class, that class or its superclass may be a subclass of Object. Anywhay, the point is, somewhere along the line, if you keep looking for a class's superclass, and that class's superclass, and so on, you will eventually get to the Object class. The Object class has many, many, subclasses, but no superclass. In fact, even all the classes in the libraries are subclasses of Object. Every class is a descendant of Object. As a result, every class inherits the public and protected methods of Object.

String toString ()

toString () is a method of Object. This method simply returns a string representation of the object. In the Object class, this returns the class name (Object), the '@' character, and the toHexString() method called on the hash code. You should just know for now that a hash code is like another identifier used for an object generated by the method. Different objects have different hash codes, and an object has one and only one hash code. This is used to differentiate different objects of the same class. Here's an example of what the toString () method may return if you call it on a new object. Note that this will differ from object to object due to different hash codes, so do not expect the same results.

java.lang.Object@15db9742

Object clone ()

This object simply returns a copy of the object that called the method. However, these two objects are different. Even though they share most of the same fields, they have differences. For example, a clone of an object has a different hash code than the original object. The clone and the object are two different objects, not a single object under different identifiers. If you clone an object and then change its value, then the same action will not be done to its clone.

Input:

```
class clone1 {
    public static void main (String[] args) {
        Object[] o = new Object[3];
        Object[] p = o.clone();


        o[0] = new Object();


        System.out.println(o[0]);
        System.out.println(p[0]);
    }
}
```

Output:

```
java.lang.Object@1175e2db
null
```

This shows how o[o] is different from p[o].

However, this is not the same if you assign a new identifier to an object.

Input:

8 Libraries

```
class clone2 {

    public static void main (String[] args) {

        Object[] o = new Object[3];

        Object[] p = o;


        o[0] = new Object();


        System.out.println(o[0]);

        System.out.println(p[0]);

    }

}
```

Output:

```
java.lang.Object@1175e2db

java.lang.Object@1175e2db
```

This shows that o[o] and p[o] refer to the same object.

These are two separate things.

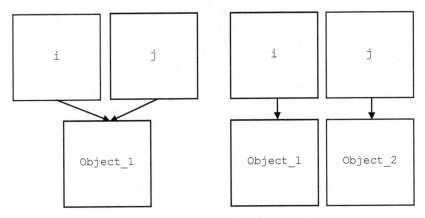

Applets

What are Applets?

Applets are just small applications. They are usually focused on accomplishing a small task, such as a calculation. Unlike the rest of the programs you have written so far in Java, Applets are run by Applet Viewers or in Web Browsers. When programming with Applets, you can manipulate what appears in the applet, including color, text, buttons, and more. I find programming with Appletsto particularly fun because you get to immediately see a visual consequence for the code you write.

Applets in Java

Java unsurprisingly has a class that you can use to create an applet. There is actually a whole package devoted to Applets called java.applet. Most notably, it has a class called Applet. You can make an applet by inheriting from Applet (i.e. making a subclass of it).

No main method

Unlike almost all programs in Java, you do not need a main method in order to run an applet. Programs that subclass Applet are special, and are run using an Applet Viewer. Instead of using a main method, you override some methods in Applet, such as init () and paint (Graphics g). The JVM starts the program at a method called init (), which is where the applet is set up. These methods will be covered shortly.

start (), stop (), and destroy ()

start (), stop (), and destroy () are three methods of the Applet class (all void return type) that care of getting the applet started and cleaning up after it is terminated. You do not have to worry about having to call these methods at the right time; they are automatically called by the browser or applet viewer when the time comes. start () is called when the applet is run, stop () is called when the applet is done running, and destroy () is called when you kill the window holding the applet.

You may override these methods if you wish to do so. For example, if you want to flash the screen every time someone opens the Applet after minimizing it, you can override the start () method.

Imports

To get started with Applets in Java, you have to import the class of a few packages for graphics. These include java.applet and java.awt. java.applet contains the class Applet. java.awt contains classes such as Graphics (used by the paint method) and ActionListener (to respond to user input via applet components, such as a button press). The Abstract Window Toolkit also comes in handy a lot when programming Applets because they contain utilities such as buttons, text fields, text areas, check boxes, information about the cursor, and more. In addition, you also probably want to import the classes of the java.awt.event package as well. This comes in handy when an event occurs, like the clicking of a button or the checking of a checkbox. It could even be as little as a mouse click. In summary, it responds to user-generated events.

java.applet

Applets have five methods that you override for the applet to function the way you want it to. They include init(), start(), stop(), destroy(), and paint(). These are all called by the applet after specific events.

Initialization: init ()

Initialization occurs when the applet is first opened. This method usually contains the code to set up an applet, including loading, text and images, and setting the parameters of the applet. This only occurs once in the applet's life: when the applet is started.

The method looks like this.

```
public void init () {

    //code for initializing the applet

}
```

Starting: start ()

This method is called after initialization or when the applet is revisited in a web page. The method for this function looks like this.

```
public void start() {

    //code for starting the applet

}
```

Stopping: stop ()

An applet is stopped when interrupted. For example, if the applet window is minimized, the stop function needs to be called because the applet is no longer wanted on the screen. This method is also called when you close the applet window. Here is the method outline for stopping an applet.

```
public void stop() {

    //code for stopping the applet
```

```
}
```

Destroying: destroy ()

Destroying an applet simply means cleaning up after the applet is closed. If there are any threads to be stopped or other changes to be made, this method is the place for it. Generally, it is best to leave this method not overridden, unless there is a purpose in mind. Here is the outline of the method.

```
public void destroy () {

    //code for destroying the applet

}
```

Painting: paint (Graphics g)

When you paint an applet, you simply draw something on the screen. This is called every time something changes in the applet, such as during an animation, or when it has to be opened after minimization. This method is called automatically and takes a parameter of the class Graphics. Graphics is just an object that can manipulate what is shown in the Applet. because in order for anything to be painted on the screen of the applet, you need access to the screen of the class and the methods of the object that can be used to change what is on the screen. In order to use this as a parameter "java.awt.Graphics" must be imported. To learn more about the Graphics class, visit the API Specification by Oracle for the Java language.

Here is the code for painting an applet.

```
public void paint (Graphics g) {

    //code for painting the applet

}
```

My First Applet!

Now that we have learned all the methods of creating the applet, let's take it one step further. Let's create our very own applet. If you are using Eclipse, you will be asked by Eclipse whether you want to run the program as an applet or as an application. Since we are creating an applet, be sure to click applet.

In our first applet, we will not do anything drastic. We will just create a new window with the text "My First Applet" in large letters in the color blue. Let's get started with the program.

Firstly, in order to draw a String on the applet, we need a font. In Java, there is a class called "Font" which contains information such as the font, font size, and font style. And to make the script blue, we need to use a field of the class "Color". So, for this applet we need to import "java.awt.Graphics", "java.awt.Font", and "java.awt.Color". AWT is a library that will be covered in this chapter.To set the font, set the color, and write the text we need to use methods of Graphics, as you can see below. The only method that we need to override in this case is paint() because we are only writing text on the screen.

```java
import java.awt.Graphics;

import java.awt.Font;

import java.awt.Color;


public class myfirstapplet extends java.applet.Applet {

    Font text_font = new Font("Arial", Font.PLAIN, 50);

    /*this creates a new object of "Font" with font in "Arial"
of size 50 in plain style*/


    public void paint(Graphics g) {


        g.setFont(text_font);
```

```
        /*this sets the font of the graphics to the object of
the class "Font" we created earlier*/

        g.setColor(Color.blue);

        /*this sets the color of the graphics to blue so that
the text is printed as blue*/

        g.drawString("My First Applet", 50, 100);

        /*finally, this draws the string "My First Applet" 50
pixels from the left, and 100 pixels from the top*/

    }

}
```

java.awt

What is the Abstract Window Toolkit?

The Abstract Window Toolkit (AWT) is just a collection of classes that are used when working with graphics. This is a package (java.awt) that covers a wide range of classes related to Graphical User Interfaces. GUIs are a means by which the user can communicate with a program. GUIs usually take place in the form of windows.

AWT has several classes that provide information about the user. For example, the AWT can tell you if the user clicks the mouse or presses a key. The AWT is also responsible for providing components such as Buttons and Checkboxes that can be used in frames. Border Layouts are also provided to help organize components.

The AWT is often a big helper when it comes to creating Applets and Java applications.

Layout Managers

A layout manager simply organizes components on a container. Before we learn more about layout managers, let's understand what those two terms mean.

What is a Component?

A component is an object in Java (java.awt.Component) that can be displayed on the screen. There are several things that can be displayed on the screen, including pictures, text, text fields, and checkboxes. Components are the things that are organized using layout managers.

What is a Container?

A container (java.awt.Container) is a type of component that is responsible for holding other components. An example is a frame. A frame is an example of a container that can hold several components. A layout manager is responsible for arranging the components of a container.

What are Layout Managers?

Layout managers help the programmer organize the location of components on a frame. Examples of components include text areas, buttons, and check boxes. When you add these components to an applet or frame, you do not have to specify their location. If you do not wish to keep the components in a specific location, but still maintain their organization, you can use layout managers. A layout simply refers to the organization of different components on the screen. In Java, the class for border layouts is called BorderLayout (careful with the capitalization). Java's libraries already have several border layouts created for you, the programmer. They all implement an interface called LayoutManager. Border layouts are used by containers. Containers are simply things that hold components (buttons, check boxes). Applets and frames are both examples of containers. In order to give your container a border layout, use the setLayout method of the Container class. This allows you to create a Layout that you want. Each of the layouts in Java are discussed below.

Flow Layout (java.awt.FlowLayout)

A flow layout is a layout in which the components "flow" in a specific direction. You can think of this as someone is writing a letter. When you write a letter, you place words starting on the left and you move right. When there is no more space left on the page, you move on to the next line. This uses the same concept.

It adds components right in the center of the screen. When another component has to be added, it is added on one side (you can choose which side) of the other button. If there is no more space next to the first button, then it is added to the next line.

Line Alignment

You can decide the direction of the flow by using a method called setAlignment (int align). This command takes in an integer value, which translates to a direction on how to align the components in a container. Based on the integer value, a flow layout is set up as either left, right, center, leading, or trailing. For example, if you wanted to center the components on the screen, then you would write setAlignment (FlowLayout.LEFT);. These integer values are found as static variables in the class java.awt.FlowLayout.

Left (FlowLayout.LEFT)

This starts the flow from the left of the screen.

Right (FlowLayout.RIGHT)

This starts the flow from the right of the screen.

Center (FlowLayout.CENTER)

This flow centers the components on the screen.

Leading (FlowLayout.LEADING)

This depends on the component's orientation. If it is a left to right orientation, then the layout starts from the left. If it is a right to left orientation, the flow starts from the right. To find out the orientation of a component, use two methods. First you need to get the ComponentOrientation object. To do this, you can use the getComponentOrientation() method of Component. This returns a ComponentOrientation object. To find out the orientation of this object, you can use the isLeftToRight() method of that object. This returns a boolean value. If the orientation is left to right, it returns true. If it is right to left, it returns false. You can also change the orientation of the component by using the setComponentOrientation (ComponentOrientation o) method of component.

Trailing (FlowLayout.TRAILING)

This depends on the component's orientation, just like the leading layout. If it is a left to right orientation, then the layout starts from the right. If it is a right to left orientation, the flow starts from the left. You can find out your component's orientation, and even change it using the getter and setter methods of a component's component orientation. Look at the section on the leading layout to find out more.

Border Layout (java.awt.BorderLayout)

A border layout organizes the components of a container toward one of five directions: north, south, east, west, and center. Unlike flow alignment in the flow layout, these fields are not integers; they are objects, specifically strings. This can be done by adding another argument with the add (Component comp) method of a panel (such as a frame or an applet). There is an overloaded version of this method that takes in another object - add (Component comp, Object restraints). That is where these directions come in. Make sure that before using this method that you have specified that you are using the border layout (using the setLayout (LayoutManager mgr) method of java.awt.Container. There are static strings for the different directions in the Border Layout (remember that strings are objects in Java, not primitive types). These static strings can be passed as the second argument of the add method. The method then takes care of placing the component in the appropriate place. If no direction is specified in the add () method, then center is used as the default direction. The five directions are BorderLayout.NORTH, BorderLayout.SOUTH, BorderLayout.WEST,

8 Libraries

BorderLayout.EAST, and BorderLayout.CENTER (they are pretty self explanatory).

Let's take a simple example. Let's say you want to add a button to the south side of a frame. Here is how you can do that.

```
import java.awt.*;


class Frame_Example {

    public static void main (String[] args) {

        Frame f = new Frame ();

        //creates a new frame

        Button b = new Button ();

        b.setLabel ("A Button");

        //creates a button titled "A Button"

        f.setLayout (new BorderLayout ());

        //sets BorderLayout as the layout of the frame

        f.add (b, BorderLayout.SOUTH);

        //adds the button to the frame at the south side


        f.setSize(100, 100);

        f.setVisible(true);

        //sets the size and visibility of the frame

    }

}
```

This layout manager is the default layout manager used unless changed to another layout manager.

Grid Layout (java.awt.GridLayout)

The Grid Layout simply involves dividing up the container into several smaller equal-sized rectangles and placing one component into each rectangle.

One constructor of this class takes two arguments to divide the container into smaller rectangles, as shown below.

```
GridLayout (int rows, int columns)
```

You can then add different components to the container.

Card Layout (java.awt.CardLayout)

The Card Layout simply arranges components in a container like cards in a stack. The first component that is added to the container is the one that is visible when the container is displayed.

Box Layout (javax.swing.BoxLayout)

This layout manager is different from the rest because unlike the others, it belongs to the package javax.swing. javax.swing is a package that contains a set of components that are used when working with AWT.

The Box Layout allows several components to be arranged along an axis (which is essentially just a line). One of the constructors takes two arguments.

```
BoxLayout (Container target, int axis)
```

The first argument indicates the container that is to contain the different components. The next takes an integer to represent the axis. These integers are static fields of BoxLayout. They include

```
BoxLayout.X_AXIS
```

This integer indicates that the different components should be placed side by side next to each other along the x-axis.

BoxLayout.Y_AXIS

This integer indicates that the different components should be placed one on top of the other along the y-axis.

BoxLayout.LINE_AXIS

This integer indicates that the different components should be arranged the same way words make up sentences. This depends on the component orientation field of the layout manager. If the component orientation is set to left to right, then the components should be arranged from left to right, the same way as the x-axis. If not, it should be arranged from top to down, like the y-axis. To find out your container's component orientation's orientation. You can find this by calling the method CONTAINER_NAME.getComponentOrientation().isLeftToRight(). This returns true if the orientation is horizontal, and false otherwise.

BoxLayout.PAGE_AXIS

This integer indicates that the different components should be arranged the same way that lines of text make up the container, which is top to down if the component orientation is set to left to right, and left to right if otherwise.

You can pass these variables that represent integers for the axis along which the components are to be aligned to the constructor. Then, you can add different components to the container and experiment with it.

Grid Bag Layout (java.awt.GridBagLayout)

The Grid Bag layout is a complex layout manager in Java that allows components of different sizes to be arranged in a container. This layout manager is more complex than the rest. Several instance variables are used when creating this layout. This book will not cover this layout manager in detail, but if you are interested, feel free to check out the online API Specification of Oracle.

Events

Events are a part of the Abstract Window Toolkit. In Java, they are related to events that occur in real life. An event is the form of communication that the Abstract Window Toolkit uses. Events have two main categories, Mouse Events, and Keyboard Events. As you can probably can guess, they have to do with how the mouse and keyboard of a computer is affected. When creating a window, we can generate events by clicking the mouse or pressing a key on the keyboard. There are several events pertaining to each.

The way we can respond to these events is by declaring methods in the class that are to be called when these events occur. The computer provides specific information, so it is important that the names and parameters of the method are the way the computer wants it to be. Here is a sample method that responds to an event. More examples are provided in Eclipse.

```
public boolean mouseDown(Event mouse_down, int x, int y) {

    System.out.println("mouse down");

    return true;

}
```

Mouse

So, what can you do with a mouse? You can click a mouse, move it around, and drag it. These all generate events in Java.

First, let's start with clicking a mouse. Believe it or not, this actually generates two events. The first one is "mouseDown", indicating that the mouse button has been pressed down. Next is "mouseUp", which means that the mouse button has been released.

Next, we can move a mouse pointer across the screen. This generates the event "mouseMove". Similarly, "mouseDrag" is generated when a mouse pointer is moved while the button is pressed.

Since the mouse pointer generates events with respect to an applet, the applet knows if the mouse is inside the frame or not. "mouseEnter" is created when the mouse enters the frame from outside, and "mouseExit" is created when the mouse exits the frame from the inside.

We could explore a lot more with mouse events, but for now it is important that you get the hang of it. Now let's move along to keyboard events.

Keyboard

Keyboards have very fewer methods, since there is less action that can be done with them. The main event done is pressing a key down. The event name is "keyDown". It has two parameters, one being the event, and the second being the integer representing the key that was pressed. Each key has a number that is then passed to the method. Just like in the mouse methods, we can respond to these events in the body of the method.

Questions

Multiple Choice

1. Which of the following is not one of Java's libraries?

    a. java.use

    b. java.util

    c. java.awt

    d. java.lang

2. Which of the following does not generate an event?

    a. Keyboard press

    b. Mouse click

    c. Mouse move

    d. Turning off the computer

3. What is used to arrange the way components are arranged in a container?

    a. superclasses

    b. layout managers

    c. Applets

    d. random number generator

4. What does int decrementExact (int a) do?

    a. Adds one to a

    b. Multiplies a by itself

    c. Takes the exact value of a

    d. Subtracts one from a

5. Which library is concerned with features of the Java language, such as classes, objects, threads, interfaces, etc.?

    a. java.util

    b. java.io

    c. java.lang

    d. java.applet

True/False

T F	The java.lang library is imported by default; the user does not have to do so manually.
T F	Libraries are collections of classes and interfaces designed to

	be used by programmers.
T F	The import statement allows the user to reference objects and interfaces of that library using a shorter name.
T F	Java's standard libraries are the only libraries available.
T F	The File class captures differences among platforms by taking an argument that represents a form on that platform.

Free Response

1. Explain what a data stream is and where it is used.

2. Compare Applets to applications.

3. What are wrapper classes and why are they used? What are their benefits?

4. Compare queues to stacks.

5. Explain what a Scanner is and how it uses delimiters to create tokens from a source.

9 PUTTING IT ALL TOGETHER

Now we have made it through most of Java's features. Let's put what we learned to use in this chapter. The goal of this chapter is to provide you with some projects you can do for practice and to clarify any confusion you may have about previously discussed concepts. This chapter tests your knowledge about Java's concepts.

Problem solving is one of the many skills required when coding, as well as logic and patience. Feel free to go back and revise previous chapters for help. However, try not to look at the solution to the problem until you think you have solved the problem or have not arrived at the solution after making a sincere effort. Hopefully, you will find these programming problems to be both fun and challenging at the same time.

Swapping Two Variables

Goal

All you have to do in this program is swap the values of two integer variables without using another variable.

Rules

- You must have a program that runs in the main method of a single class titled Swap.

- There must only be two integers in the program: a and b. The value of a should be 3, and the value of b should be 5. The declaration and assignment should look like the following.

```
int a = 3;

int b = 5;
```

- You must swap the two values of the integers without introducing a third variable. You cannot use another variable. Below is an example of what not to do.

- After you are finished, print a followed by b using a print command.

```
int a = 3;

int b = 5;

int c = a;

int a = b;
```

Hints

- This problem does have a solution.

- The solution requires you to perform each numerical operation on the two numbers and set the value of each equal to one of the variables

Sample Solution

```
public class Swap {

    public static void main (String [] args) {

        int a = 3;

        int b = 5;
```

```
    a = a + b;

    //a IS NOW 8, THE SUM OF 3 AND 5

    b = a - b;

    //b IS NOW 3, THE DIFFERENCE OF 8 AND 5

    a = a - b;

    //a IS NOW 5, TEH DIFFERENCE OF 8 AND 3


    //a IS 5, b IS 3


    System.out.println(a + " " + b);

  }

}
```

Fibonacci Sequence

Fibonacci is simply a pattern of numbers. One number of the sequence is formed from the sum of the previous two numbers. The first two numbers are 0 and 1. Their sum forms the next number, which is 1. After that comes the sum of 1 and 1, which is 2. This pattern continues as long as you want it to. Here is what the first ten numbers of the Fibonacci sequence are.

0 1 1 2 3 5 8 13 21 34

Goal

Your job is to create a program that can print out the Fibonacci sequence of a length specified by the arguments passed to the main method.

Rules

- You have to create a single-class program that can print out the Fibonacci sequence.

- The program should be entirely written inside the main method of a class called Fibonacci.

- You have to create a loop that can print the Fibonacci sequence by calculating the numbers on its own. Do not simply print the first ten numbers. Print the first 10 numbers of the Fibonacci sequence

Hints

- You need to create a for loop and print variables using the print command System.out.print (); or System.out.println ();

- You will most likely find it easier to create three variables rather than two. Two of them will store the two numbers, and the third will hold the sum of the two.

Sample Program

Now, let's write a program that can write that sequence. Since this is a procedural program (meaning that it doesn't have to do with the creation of objects), it will require only one class with a main method. That method will contain two variables and a loop, in which each number will be printed. Follow along with the program below:

```
class Fibonacci {

    public static void main (String[] args) {

        int number_1 = 0;

        int number_2 = 1;

        /*these two variables begin the pattern*/


        System.out.println(number_1);
```

```
        System.out.println(number_2);

        /*the first two numbers are printed*/


        for (int i = 0; i < 8; i++) {

            /*this is a "For" loop that repeats eight times.
The first two numbers have already been printed, and the other
eight are printed here in this loop.*/

            int number_3 = number_1 + number_2;

            /*a third number is created from the sum of the
first two*/

            System.out.println(number_3);

            /*the third number is printed*/

            number_1 = number_2;

            number_2 = number_3;

            /*The second and third number integers must be set
to the first and second number values so that the next value
can be found using the sum of the two. The loop continues to
repeat, therefore producing the next numbers of the Fibonacci
sequence.*/

        }

    }

}
```

Palindrome

A palindrome is a word or sentence that reads the same forwards as it does backwards. For the sake of this example, spaces can be ignored. For example, "taco cat" is a palindrome because if you reverse the letters (and take out the spaces), it is still "tacocat". Explaining what a palindrome to a computer is not so easy, and is somewhat tedious. In the following program, user input is given through the main method's arguments. This program asks you to write a program to identify a pallindrome, by comparing the first letter to the last letter, the second letter to the second last letter, and so on. If all these conditions are true, the word can be considered a palindrome (try it with "nurses run" or "madam"). Notice that the first letter is the same as the last letter, the second letter is the same as the second last letter, the third letter is the same as the third last letter, and so on.

Goal

Identify if a string passed though main method arguments is a palindrome, disregarding the spaces.

Rules

- Create a class called Pallindrome

- The program should be written entirely within the main method

- You must connect the elements of String [] args without spaces into a large string.

- Use the charAt[4] (int i) method to compare the first character to the last. Do the same for the second character and second last character, the third and third last character, and so on until the last two. If these all turn out to be the same, then you have a pallindrome!

---

[4] To learn more about the charAt (int i) method, visit Oracle's online API specification.

- If a pallindrome is found, print "PALLINDROME :)". If not, print "NOT PALLINDROME :(".

- Pass the following strings through the main method arguments (once for each time you run the program) and let your program identify which of the following are palindromes.

"runner"

"racecar"

"suspicious"

"gags"

"dad"

"was it a cat I saw"

Hints

- This program will require you to use loops, once for the concatenation (joining together) of the strings, and once for the pallindrome search.

Sample Program

```
public class Pallindrome {

    public static void main (String[] args) {

        boolean palindrome = false;
        /*a boolean is declared and set to false*/


        String userinput = "";

        /*a string is created to hold the user input in
a single string*/
```

```java
        for (int i = 0; i < args.length; i++) {

            userinput += args[i];

        }

        /*All the elements that are in the array are added to
the string without spaces.Essentially, the spaces are removed
from the main method arguments.*/



        for (int i = 0; i < userinput.length(); i++) {

            /*A loop is created and repeats the same number of
times as the number of letters there are in the user input.*/



            if (userinput.charAt(i) !=
userinput.charAt(userinput.length()-1-i)) {

                break;

            }

            /*This breaks the loop if the ith letter is not
equal to the ith from the last letter.*/



            if (i == userinput.length() - 1) {

                palindrome = true;

                /*If the last character has been reached and
the loop hasn't been broken yet, then the word must be a
pallindrome, so the boolean is set to true.*/

            }

        }



        if (palindrome == true) {
```

```
        System.out.println("PALLINDROME  :)");

    }

    else {

        System.out.println("NOT PALLINDROME  :(");

    }

        /*If the word is a pallindrome, "PALLINDROME  :)"
is printed; if not, "NOT PALLINDROME  :(" is printed*/

    }

}
```

Treats

There are many different kinds of treats, but they all have certain characteristics in common, such as being tasty. We can illustrate this in Java using subclasses and superclasses. The superclass "treat" will contain features that all treats have. Then, the subclasses of "treat", such as "candy" or "chips" will have all the features that "treat" has, like being tasty, but they will also contain features unique to themselves. For example, "candy" will have a variable for sugar, while "chips" won't.

Goal

Create an efficient class hierarchy of treats.

Rules

- This program requires you to make three classes, each in a separate file. Their names are candy, chips, and treat.

- candy and chips should be subclasses of the class treat.

- treat class should have a boolean field called tasty set to true. It should have an integer called calories set to o. It should also have a method called who_am_i () that returns a string equal to the name of the class, or "treat".

- Each of the subclasses should do two things: 1) assign a value to the calories field of the integer in its constructor. 2) override the who_am_i () method to return a String equal to the name of the subclass.

- Create a separate class called test to test out the features of your program. Create objects from your classes, call methods on them, and print out their properties to make sure your program works.

Sample Program

```
class treat {

    boolean tasty = true;

    /*This boolean is declared and assigned to true because
all treats are tasty.*/


    int calories = 0;

    /*This integer is declared and assigned to 0. Although all
treats have calories, the amount varies from treat to treat*/


    public String who_am_i() {

        return "treat";

    }

    /*This method returns the name of the class, and is
overridden by the subclasses*/

}
```

9 Putting it all Together

That was a fairly simple class. Now let's create the subclasses of "treat" using the "extends" keyword.

```
class candy extends treat {

    candy () {

        /*The number of calories is assigned upon the creation
of this object.*/

        calories = 50;

    }

    public String who_am_i() {

        return "candy";

    }

}

class chips extends treat {

    chips () {

        /*The number of calories is assigned upon the creation
of this object.*/

        calories = 150;

    }

    public String who_am_i() {

        return "chips";

    }

}
```

Now we have assigned a value to the calories variable that was inherited from the superclass, "treat". There are many other treats that can be used as subclasses of the "treat" class, but for now, we have only covered two to keep things simple.

From this example, we created a superclass containing a simple outline of the characteristics of all traits and an abstract method. In the subclasses, we built on those methods, and finished the body of the abstract method.

Now let's test these features out. Here is a sample test class.

```
class test {

    public static void main (String[] args) {

        //This class tests out the features of the other class.

        chips ch = new chips ();

        System.out.println (ch.who_am_i ());

        candy ca = new candy ();

        System.out.println (ca.calories);

    }

}
```

Cars

Similar to the last example, cars are also good examples of superclasses. Cars have many characteristics as well as things they can do. These can be represented as subclasses and superclasses. In addition, we will use an interface to collect all the methods that belong to cars. Let's start by creating a simple interface with two methods.

Goal

Create a class called car that implements an interface called car_actions, as well as two subclasses of car.

Rules

- Create an interface called car_van_truck_actions that contains two methods, void turn_headlight_on (); and void change_speed (int change);

- Create a class called car that implements car_van_truck_actions that has an int called speed, boolean called is_headlight_on, and String called source_of_power.

- Implement the two methods: turn_headlight_on () should set the value of is_headlight_on to true and change_speed should change the value of the speed variable by the variable in its parameter.

- Create two subclasses of car_model called electric_car and gasoline_car whose source_of_power strings are set to "Electricity" and "Gasoline" respectively.

- Create a separate class called tester to test out the features of your program. Create objects from your classes, call methods on them, and print out their properties to make sure your program works.

Sample Program

```
public interface car_van_truck_actions {

    public void turn_headlight_on();

    public void change_speed(int change);

    /*These are methods that will need to be implemented by
cars, vans, and trucks. For now, we are working with cars.*/

}
```

Now let's create the class "car_model" to implement these methods.

```
public class car_model implements car_van_truck_actions {

    int speed = 0;

    boolean is_headlight_on;
```

```
    String source_of_power;


    public void turn_headlight_on() {

        is_headlight_on = true;

    }


    public void change_speed (int change) {

        speed += change;

    }

}
```

Let's create two subclasses of "car_model", "electric_car" and "gasoline_car".

```
public class electric_car extends car_model{

    electric_car () {

        source_of_power = "Electricity";

        /*Changes the source of power variable to
"Electricity"*/

    }

}

public class gasoline_car extends car_model{

    gasoline_car () {

        source_of_power = "Gasoline";

        /*Changes the source of power variable to "Gasoline"*/

    }

}
```

9 Putting it all Together

Now, let's test these two out. Here is a sample test class.

```
class tester {

    public static void main (String [] args) {

        electric_car ec = new electric_car ();

        ec.turn_headlight_on ();

        System.out.println (ec.is_headlight_on);

        gasoline_car gc = new gasoline_car ();

        gc.change speed (1);

        System.out.println (gc.source_of_power);

    }

}
```

Index

ABOUT THE AUTHOR

Ravit Sharma developed a passion for programming since an early age when he was in elementary school. He is familiar with programming languages such as JavaScript, C#, Scratch, Python, and Terrapin Logo. He has also done several projects using the Raspberry Pi, a pocket-sized computer. Ravit completed a Java programming course developed by Stanford University.

Currently Ravit is a high school sophomore and also working part time at a private educational institute. He loves to stay involved with the community. For the last four years he has been volunteering as a commissioner in his city's Youth Advisory Commission.

www.ingramcontent.com/pod-product-compliance
Lightning Source LLC
LaVergne TN
LVHW022306060326
832902LV00020B/3308